FLIPPING THE SCRIPT

THE PSYCHOLOGY OF DOOR-TO-DOOR SALES

COBI BEAL

Are you interested in bulk purchases of this book for your team or company?

Contact me for a discount schedule

cdhbeal@gmail.com

...

LinkedIn – Cobi Beal

Matthew 7:7

TABLE OF CONTENTS

INTRODUCTION

Have you realized that the script, rebuttals and closes only account for half of what it takes to be great at door-to-door sales? Knowing when to utilize these things is needed, but it doesn't account for the psychological foundation of selling directly to homeowners. This is why some reps perform a lot better than others, even when they're using the same script.

You will drastically increase your odds of creating productive sales dialogue (and closing) if you attain a positive snap judgment from the homeowner.

Imagine the homeowner's perspective. This isn't the 1950s anymore. People are rarely excited to hear somebody knock at their door unannounced. The homeowner is likely working, watching a show, getting ready to go somewhere, dealing with a family matter or at least doing something to keep themselves busy. So, when they go to their front door and see someone who appears to be a solicitor, they instantly become primed with annoyance and/or skepticism before any words have even been said.

What most scripts and teachings don't explain is that your introduction needs to flip the homeowner's event schema just as much as it needs to hook their interest.

Social psychology has found that we as humans build cognitive 'schemas' that help us quickly identify the world around us. A schema is simply a mental shortcut to help us recognize how we should think or act in situations that are familiar to us.

For example, a homeowner's mental shortcut to seeing a well-dressed stranger knock on their door is usually to think 'solicitor,' and then resort to whatever they've programmed themselves to do (e.g., hide under their windowsill, open their door just to say 'no soliciting,' say whatever necessary to get you to leave, etc.).

This is specifically called an 'event schema,' and most homeowners already negatively qualify both you and the situation before you have a fighting chance to convince them otherwise. So, the logical first question you must ask yourself is, "How do I flip their event schema and create a positive snap judgment?"

The only way to successfully do this with homeowners is by barraging them with multiple pieces of evidence that collectively disarm their existing mental shortcut.

This means that you need to dress, act and address the homeowner in ways that are uniquely different than what they expect. Failure to do so within the first few seconds will increase the odds of you being blatantly rejected. But besides attaining a positive snap judgment, most door-to-door reps aren't taught how to *maintain* a positive snap judgment.

They aren't taught the basics of engaging homeowners in sales dialogue and mutual conversation, which are both important for building interest and rapport.

Mere script memorization will not teach door-to-door reps the psychological framework that caters to the tentative nuances of quick solicitations. There are too many variables involved that need to be clearly understood. This also includes the art of pleasant persistence during the back half of the sale. Homeowners will usually say 'no' at least once before they ever say 'yes,' so reps need to know how to push through 'no' multiple times without seeming pushy or desperate.

You can easily double your closing rate by implementing validation and reciprocity as you resolve, ace and close multiple times.

The goal of this book is to help you implement influential psychology into each part of your pitch. In addition, it will provide a multidimensional perspective that will cater to various situations, and reduce your risk of being a stereotypical solicitor.

CHAPTER 1:

TO SELL IS TO COUNSEL

og covered the grounds of the psychiatric hospital. It wasn't a hard decision for the patient to run, so it came as no surprise to me when his body disappeared into the fog.

Although the interior of our buildings were as lockdown as it could get, the outside looked more like a middle-school campus. The irony of this became more and more apparent each time I had to chase down a fleeing patient. It was still our job to be rehabilitative, though. We would still risk bringing 'safe' patients outside.

By the time another staff member and I caught up with the one who ran, we were close to the city street. We had to restrain him into the wet grass as he struggled to get free. Unbeknownst to us, while he was on the ground, fighting, the patient had grabbed a golf-ball-sized rock. We kept this struggle up for ten minutes until security pulled up in their car. I was already exhausted and feeling the cold air rip through my lungs by the time they got there, but we still had to restrain the patient into the back of the security car, and then inside to the seclusion room.

At the hospital, we were not allowed to use mechanical restraints (i.e., handcuffs), so the two of us held the patient's arms and legs as we stuffed ourselves into the back of the car. I think you'd be surprised how hard it is to do this when a patient is trying to struggle to break free.

As soon as security started driving, the patient got his arm free from the other staff member. He slammed the rock he had been hiding into my left eyebrow, and then sunk his teeth into the forearm of the other staff member. It took some maneuvering, but we detached the biting patient and got ourselves situated by the time we pulled up to the building. From there, we had to climb out of the car while still restraining the patient. It took quite a bit longer, but eventually, we got him locked inside of the seclusion room.

You might be wondering why I'm telling you this story, since you're probably never going to restrain a homeowner for their credit card. But the best reason I can give for telling you this is so that I can paint you a picture of the type of environment that taught me how to sell. Believe me, there is some hardcore 'selling' that takes place in psychiatric hospitals.

Imagine trying to convince a psychologically, emotionally and behaviorally distressed teenager to walk themselves into a seclusion room without putting up a fight. Sometimes, it would work, and sometimes, it wouldn't. I have human bite scars as proof of what happened in times when it didn't.

It was my job to manage and support high-risk teenagers in one of the most lock-down/restrictive youth psychiatric hospitals in the country. Since it was 'psychiatric' care, the patients were never locked inside their bedrooms; they had the physical ability to come out any time they wanted. Although restraints and seclusions were necessary on a daily basis, the best staff members were the ones who were able to use their de-escalation skills to avoid these incidents in the first place.

As far-fetched as it sounds, there is quite a bit of overlap between de-escalating a psychiatric patient and selling something to a homeowner on their doorstep. The good news here is, you don't have to work at a psychiatric hospital to gain that understanding.

There's an art to approaching somebody who doesn't want to talk to you.

The idea is simple, and it's that homeowners typically become annoyed by your knocking, and then even more annoyed if you jump right into a stereotypical sales pitch. This immediately repels homeowners. They become awkward and/or annoyed, and then seek to get rid of you as quickly as possible.

Most first-year reps get cut off, interrupted or quickly rejected before they're able to 'get through a full pitch,' and as a result, they become discouraged. They're not taught to prioritize first impressions and productive sales dialogue.

You have to first ask yourself, "How am I going to get the homeowner to even listen to me? What about my introduction is going to disarm them and also hook their interest?"

The answer to these questions goes a lot deeper than *what* you say. In door-to-door sales dialogue, the majority of the selling isn't about you explaining the perks and benefits of your product/service. You have to first build the rapport and interest that earns you the right to talk about that stuff. If done correctly, you won't be portrayed as a stereotypical solicitor. You'll earn the right to pitch, talk about price, resolve true concerns and close without reinforcing the homeowner's opinion of you just trying to make a commission.

At the psychiatric hospital, patients often hated the staff members who didn't empathize with their situation or learn about their point of view, and consequently, the patients were less likely to follow typical directions that those staff members gave. It's easy to just give orders, but what happens when the patient becomes escalated and you don't have the rapport to calm them down? How are you supposed to get the patient to even listen to you if you haven't validated their situation and portrayed a sense of empathy?

This is similar to door-to-door sales. How are you supposed to get the homeowner to even listen to you if you haven't empathetically generated a positive first impression? And then how are you supposed to generate interest if you haven't taken the time to listen to the homeowner and learn how to cater your pitch accordingly?

By the way, I'm not talking about fake rapport. I'm not talking about the NFL team flag - that just so happens to be 'your favorite team' as well - hanging above their garage. Homeowners will see right through that.

What I'm talking about is the type of rapport that's built when you've perfected your introduction and successfully generated a mutual (relevant) conversation.

This will significantly raise the amount of actual sales conversations that homeowners allow you to engage them in.

The truth is, reps are almost always underprepared because they're not taught how to earn the right to get to this point. They get hit with a rude awakening as they consistently encounter negative event schemas that they don't know how to flip.

Traditional training puts too much emphasis on rote-rehearsing a script that doesn't fully account for the perspective of the homeowner.

Every door-to-door rep needs to have perfected an introduction that seamlessly transitions into a purposeful question. This will make it easier to generate productive sales dialogue, and will end up going a lot further than rushing into the perks and benefits of whatever you're selling.

Even Screamers Can Be Buyers

"Are you blind or can you just not read? The damn sign says no soliciting!" He pointed a stiff finger at a very faint sign that read, 'No Soliciting.'

This was my second screamer of the day so far. Obviously, he had built up a strong event schema for solicitors. The man was probably in his 40s. He was bald, had bloodshot eyes, and wore an unbuttoned dress shirt with the collar popped up.

I only had one quick shot to flip his snap judgment. "Sir, give me the boot anytime, but actually, the reason I'm here is because I'm the bug and rodent guy for some of your neighbors. You probably know John next door, right?"

The man paused for a moment before replying, "Yeah, why?"

"I'm gonna be helping him out with the sugar ants and the mice. What do you do about that stuff?"

We then had a conversation about his current pest situation. I didn't mention that I was selling anything until he specifically asked, and after considerable negotiation, he actually bought a one-year plan. At the end of the sale, the man looked at me and said, "Sorry for yelling, I thought you were like one of those other solicitors. They've been ridiculous this year."

My response to his initial outburst was not foolproof. Most people like this are likely to still reject any attempt to challenge their perspective, but this guy happened to be the type to feel cognitive dissonance and rescind his original snap judgment.

But the bottom line is, the sale never would have been made if I hadn't had the confidence to try, and if I didn't have the certainty that I was more than just a solicitor.

In times like this, referencing yourself to neighbors can create cognitive dissonance within homeowners who are disrespectful or blatantly annoyed. They feel bad about their outburst because they feel like they were mean to a friend of a friend. Mentioning neighbors is something that I will shed more light on later. I'm sure that you already know the importance of this part, but there are specific (alternative) ways to utilize the names of nearby neighbors that are important to elaborate on.

Although the typical homeowner is not as angry or blatantly disrespectful as this example, you will almost always have to challenge their existing event schema before they've finalized their snap judgment of you. After successfully doing so, this gives you a window of opportunity to create productive sales dialogue. It also goes to show that a homeowner's initial demeanor doesn't automatically categorize their likelihood of buying.

Positively challenging, engaging, listening and catering to the person you're talking with will end up going a lot further than jumping straight into a rehearsed 'cut-and-paste' pitch.

Immediately pitching is the quickest way to get tuned out or cut off. Instead of pitching immediately, earn the right to pitch; this means that you've made a good first impression and you've engaged them into mutual sales dialogue. Engaging the homeowner into a mutual conversation will help you clarify their interest level, and then help you learn more about their unique situation. This way, you won't waste time with non-buyers, and you won't give a boring 'one-size-fits-all' pitch to potential buyers.

In door-to-door sales, your introduction needs to be concise, meaningful and rid of useless information so that you can create this conversation as quickly as possible.

Homeowners are hyper-attuned to notice red flags. They're also prone to tune you out or quickly cut you off, so perfecting your introduction is absolutely needed. However, perfecting the introduction is actually the second goal in a sale. The first goal needs to be accomplished before you even knock on a door.

CHAPTER 2:

YOU NEED TO PICK THE HOMEOWNER'S LOCK

Do you remember learning how to open an old-fashioned, spinning combination lock? It probably took you a while to consistently get it right. First, you have to memorize the combination, and you also have to memorize how many times to spin the knob and in which direction.

Just like there are multiple numbers to open a lock, likewise, there are multiple 'sales' that need to be made in order to close a deal. There are multiple numbers or 'clicks' that must be accomplished in order to get what you want. Unlike a lot of books, I'm not going to make you read until the end to know the full story, so, here you go. There are four main objectives or 'sales' that need to be made.

You have to sell yourself, sell the homeowner, sell the product/service and then close the deal.

The first sale happens before you even talk to a home-owner. The first sale is all about building and maintaining a positive, confident and productive mentality. Don't over-look this part. It has more significance than you can imag-ine, especially if you haven't done door-to-door already.

The second sale happens approximately in the first five seconds of meeting a potential customer. They must be sold on you being unique and/or beneficial rather than you being 'just another solicitor.' Your success rate will be strongly correlated with attaining this positive snap judgment.

The third sale is about maintaining this positive snap judgment, as well as the rapport that you actively build. This is important for keeping momentum throughout the sales dialogue. The homeowner must feel as though you're seeking to understand and help them rather than just seek-ing a commission.

The fourth sale is the final sale. It's about knowing how to validate, resolve, ace and close the deal while being pleas-antly persistent. Specific psychological factors need to be implemented in order to push through 'no' multiple times.

What's important to understand is that you will rarely get to sale number four without successfully get-ting through sales one, two and three.

Here are some last few things I'd like to mention be-fore getting into more detail:

1) Most of the advice I give is backed by psychological findings.

   The advice is also backed by personal experience from door-to-door sales and the psychiatric hospital. Although some of what I recommend is up for debate, I guarantee that it provides valuable insight and will be beneficial for the vast majority of those who apply it.

2) My door-to-door experience was in residential pest control, so that's what my examples will mostly relate to.

   Nonetheless, the insight that I give is easily applicable to other types of sales as well. Inasmuch as I will try to be as general as possible, there are examples and anecdotes that cater to my specific experiences.

3) This book is less about script-building and more about building a psychological framework around your script.

   It will dive into how the pitch needs to be chopped up and uniquely pieced together after the introduction. This is how you engage the homeowner and then cater to their unique situation. The script should be memorized and utilized accordingly, but what you'll learn is that a script isn't a multidimensional formula.

In other words, you need to build a framework that allows you to prioritize the interaction.

People buy with emotion and then justify with logic. It's almost always better to rely on the experience that you provide rather than a script by itself.

A script is more of a recommended guideline that should be cherry-picked from, not rehearsed. There are multiple aspects and dimensions of door-to-door sales interactions that couldn't possibly all fit into a single script.

Your introduction is the only thing that will almost never change. Other than giving off the right first impression, using the exact same introduction will help you disclose the homeowner's interest level and unique situation. Then you can build a conversation and cater your pitch. I'll elaborate on this later.

Sales Funnel

The sales funnel is a metaphor that I will mention throughout the book. Think of a funnel that's out in the rain. The bigger the funnel is, the more raindrops it will catch.

Your goal is to expand your sales 'funnel,' inch by inch, every single day.

The important thing to remember is that the advice and strategies that I give are not foolproof. However, they will inevitably provide a higher percentage of success to anyone who implements them. What this book aims to do is 'raise your batting average.'

As you talk to homeowners, the goal is to mindfully notice the situations that can be improved on. Even the best reps get told 'no' a lot more than they're told 'yes,' but what makes the great reps better than others is their ability to learn from rejection and create an opportunity to grow their sales funnel.

You might talk to one hundred 'decision makers' in a single day and be told 'yes' only once, or never even get a 'yes' at all. This constant state of rejection is the biggest underlying reason why so many people quit, or never even try door-to-door sales.

But at the end of the day, what you'll learn is that the secret to success in this line of work lies in the ability to stay positive, to stay hungry and to stay in a constant state of learning, because nobody gets good overnight; they just learn how to grow their sales funnel one day at a time.

CHAPTER 3:
SELLING YOURSELF TO YOURSELF

Do you eat your vegetables before, during or after eating the other parts of the dinner? I eat them first just to get them out of the way. Although they're not usually the most enjoyable, they're usually the most beneficial. Think of this chapter as the vegetables of the book. Controlling your mindset and 'selling yourself to yourself' are probably the most important parts of preparation before you can begin knocking doors.

In other words, I want you to eat your vegetables now before I bring out the steak and potatoes.

The Cognitive Triangle

Door-to-door selling is a lot like having the courage to start a spontaneous conversation with an attractive person at a party. The more relaxed and confident you are, the better at it you'll be.

Before talking to a stranger or a homeowner, your mindset needs to be prepared and established.

Think of it this way – what's your success rate going to be if you have low confidence, are fearful, and feel like a nuisance? Unfortunately, you're most likely going to be nervous when you first start — that's almost inevitable. Although the nerves go away quickly, they can easily turn into negative thoughts and feelings if you haven't prepared your mentality. Nobody is great when they first start, so you need to focus your attention on controlling the things that are actually controllable.

The most important thing for you to control is called your 'cognitive triangle.' If you don't learn how to control this, then it will start controlling you.

This is the most relevant psychological understanding when preparing your mindset to sell. The cognitive triangle is most associated with Cognitive Behavioral Therapy (CBT). It seeks to help individuals understand how their thoughts, emotions and actions are all connected, and how they actively influence one another.

Imagine a triangle. The top point represents 'thoughts,' the bottom right point represents 'emotions,' and the bottom left point represents 'actions.'

Here is a general example of how this works — a person has the thought that they're unattractive or unlikable, therefore, they experience the emotion of feeling sad or unwanted, so, they actively choose to stay home instead of going out to seek friends or a potential partner. Similarly, for the positive — a person thinks that they're attractive or likable, therefore, they feel good or desirable, so, they actively go out to seek friends or a potential partner.

On your first day of door-to-door (for those who haven't knocked yet), you're going to drive into an unfamiliar neighborhood, and the reality of what you signed up for is going to really sink in. For a lot of new reps, they never fully imagined what it's going to be like to walk up to a random house, knock on the door and convince a stranger to buy something. Other than script memorization, they haven't prepared for the dynamic rapport and influence involved in getting the homeowner to buy and disclose payment information. On top of this, most new reps haven't prepared for how they're going to handle the continuous rejection that follows.

On day one, it's natural to get hit with negative *thoughts*. It's common to *feel* nervous, doubtful and/ or incapable. Then it becomes easy to *act* this way as soon as doors get opened.

And the worst part is that most homeowners are going to sense this and likely be repelled by your awkward or nervous presence. They will be more likely to cut you off, slam their door in your face or tell you 'No soliciting.'

Now, this is not to turn you off, as my goal is not to turn you away from door-to-door sales; my aim here is to prepare you for the reality of it. And the good news is, you can build up the required confidence by having a clearer understanding of the relevant psychology. Simply put, if you stay positive, you will more likely give good first impressions and control snap judgments. Try to not oversimplify the fact that we're naturally able to read other people's emotional state, and we're attracted to happy and confident people.

Your cognitive triangle will subconsciously affect the homeowner as well, making them more likely to think, feel and act in a way that's either beneficial or detrimental to the sale.

Later on, I'll dive much deeper into influencing first impressions, maintaining first impressions and naturally closing sales, but first, it's vital for every door-to-door sales rep to understand how to prepare their thoughts and emotions before taking the action of knocking doors.

The Four Truths

Your first goal needs to be to sell yourself (and your product/service) *to yourself*. This means that you have 100% convinced yourself of four things:

1) That your product/service is great and offers quality value.

   If you don't like what you're selling, it's hard to convince others to buy it. A good question to ask yourself is, "Would I actually buy this?" If your answer is 'yes,' then the next question you want to ask yourself is, "Would I buy this from myself?"

You want to first make sure that you sound confident and certain, so that you don't have to fake it.

Faking it will keep you from sounding enthusiastic and confident in your value proposition. It will also make it harder to push through 'no,' when you get towards the end of the sale. More importantly, it will be harder to be pleasantly persistent if you don't believe that it'll be genuinely beneficial to the homeowner.

Everything from your tone of voice, your facial expressions to your body language will naturally work in your favor when you're completely sold on the quality of what you're offering.

Can you remember the last time you believed something so strongly (the quality of a movie, your religion, your innocence to a guilty accusation, or something of those sorts) that you barely needed to use any words to convey your message? You likely spoke clearly and certainly, fluctuated the speed and volume of your voice, and looked straight into the eyes of the other person. The confidence and certainty oozed out of your pores.

Although you're not going to always talk like this, this is the type of confidence and certainty that you need to manifest (especially in your introduction). People will subconsciously pick up on it and perceive your offer as something of high value.

2) You are confident that every person will want to buy your offer (or at least want to hear about it). This is also referred to as 'assuming the sale.'

Even though your closing ratio is going to be low when you first start, you have to always assume that each homeowner is a potential buyer (but you cannot be negatively affected by rejection). Your thoughts, emotions and actions will start working against you if you let rejection get to your head.

However, when you stay positive and continuously assume each sale, you will embody a stronger sense of confidence and authority that allows you to *create* more sales.

3) You're never a nuisance to anybody you talk to. With respect to door-to-door sales, you're a benefit to the neighborhood as a whole.

In every single neighborhood, there are always a couple of people (at least) who want/need what you're offering. But if you're not portraying confidence and positivity on each doorstep, you'll miss out on those sales. Think of it this way – you're actually doing a disservice to the people who want or need your offer. Your negative mentality will prevent them from attaining a valued benefit to their lives, and the worst part is that they'll probably buy from the next door-to-door rep that confidently knocks on their door and offers the same product/service.

Regardless of how many times you're yelled at, cussed at or disrespected on the doors, the truth is, you owe your composure to the potential buyers just as much as you owe it to yourself.

Homeowners do not buy based on what you say; they buy based on *the interaction* and the energy that you bring. Positivity and confidence will make them more willing to open up and engage in authentic sales dialogue.

4) You're an expert, and you deserve respect from every single person you encounter.

This doesn't mean that you get into arguments or that you engage in negativity. What this means is that you embody a sense of authority and expertise. You always hold yourself in high regard, regardless of the way you're treated. You're the bigger person, and you walk away from blatant disrespect, but you also have the genuine belief that *they are wrong* for perceiving you in a negative way to begin with.

You have the confidence to challenge snap judgments. You have the common sense to know when it's best to apologize and walk away. You have the ability to never let anyone negatively affect your cognitive triangle.

This mindset will help get you into authentic sales dialogue more often. Think of it like this – your job is to stay positive as you filter out 'nos' all day, so that you are ready when you finally run into the people who are more likely to say 'yes.' Convince yourself that you are not a solicitor or a nuisance. Nobody wants to buy from a solicitor or a nuisance. It's your first 'sale' to convince yourself that you're neither of these things.

Although the other person will probably try to identify you as such, you have the power to disprove their event schema and then manipulate their snap judgment before it's too late. This is the second 'sale' about selling yourself (and your credibility) to the other person, and it all starts with your mentality.

CHAPTER 4:
SELLING YOURSELF TO THE HOMEOWNER

I hope that you never have to physically restrain a violent person who has butter rubbed all over their arms. It's not the most enjoyable activity, especially during the evening shift at a psychiatric hospital.

Two patients had attacked a staff member at the exact same time. It usually took two to four staff members to restrain a single patient (who didn't have buttered arms), so I'm sure you can imagine how this unit was doing with just the five people who were on shift that evening.

I still remember the 'show of support' that they called for over the radio. You could always tell the intensity of the situation based on the background noise and the frantic nature of the person's voice. I had just started working at the hospital. On this particular day, I was wearing baggy sweatpants and a baggy sweatshirt. I was not wearing my badge, and my radio was deep in my pocket rather than clipped on to a visible spot. I ran over to where the unit's door had been propped open for responding staff members. But just as I got a few steps away, a staff member stepped in my path and purposefully blocked me from getting past. He stepped forward to try to grab me, but then did a double take as he realized that I was a worker, not a patient. My appearance had made him qualify me incorrectly.

This is called a 'snap judgment,' and in this particular circumstance, it did not work in my favor. When the staff member saw me running up to the door, he had only a couple seconds to decide who I was, and then act on that decision. Contributing variables included the fact that I was a new face, I was not dressed like a worker, and the staff member was likely primed with the stress of the situation.

Studies vary on the exact number, but on average, it's proven that we make snap judgments about people within the first four or five seconds of meeting them.

This number likely shrinks even further in door-to-door sales. Put yourself in the shoes of the homeowner. Imagine being busy at home when you hear a knock or the doorbell ring. You get up and see a well-dressed stranger standing on the other side of your door. Most homeowners will already resort to their negative event schema, but you still have a few seconds to flip it to your favor.

As soon as they open their door, they will be hyper-attuned to every single detail in how you present yourself.

They will fall victim to their own confirmation bias, so every aspect of your presentation needs to be perfected. Small details that are unaccounted for can easily portray you as being a stereotypical solicitor. This will land you a negative snap judgment, and make the homeowner only think about how to get you to leave as quickly and as easily as possible.

The truth is, although we're taught to not judge books by their cover, we do. It's evolutionarily advantageous to quickly assess our environment and make snap judgments about whether we should fight, flee or relax.

Schemas are a cognitive shortcut to help us generalize situations in order to make accurate snap judgments with less cognitive effort. This is exactly what's going on when a homeowner lays eyes on you.

How to Sell Like Will Ferrell

What would happen if Will Ferrell did door-to-door sales? Do you think he would do well? Of course, he would. Most people know and love Will Ferrell. Most people would immediately associate him as part of their 'in' group and assume that all of his intentions have positive attributions.

Unfortunately, I can't promise that you'll magically look like Will Ferrell when knocking doors, but I can promise that you'll understand how to utilize the psychological understanding of how people categorize one another.

We as humans categorize individuals either 'in' our social group (belonging) or 'out' of our social group (not belonging), and homeowners will be very quick to categorize you.

'In' group members are perceived as unique individuals within the group, whereas, 'out' group people are perceived as stereotypical and 'all the same.' And unfortunately for you, you have the homeowner's event schema working against you. Once we're categorized as either 'in' group or 'out' group, another social psychology finding comes into play. It is called the 'fundamental attribution bias.'

Here's an example of how this bias in our thinking works - imagine that you're late for a meeting. You're much more likely to attribute your tardiness to an external reason rather than internal (e.g., traffic). You usually make the same attributions for others who you perceive as being part of your 'in' group. But when it comes to people who you perceive as 'out' group, you would attribute their tardiness to something internal (e.g., poor time management).

So, when the homeowner answers their door, they make a snap judgment of you in a matter of seconds. This then becomes a lens that reveals biases and how they perceive your solicitation.

If they perceive you as 'out' group (as a stereotypical solicitor), they'll attribute your solicitation to negative reasons. They'll probably think that you'll 'say anything to make a commission.'

However, if they perceive you as 'in' group, they'll attribute your solicitation to positive reasons. They'll probably think that you actually take care of their neighbors and are more of a 'good news messenger.'

Perfecting your introduction will raise your odds of attaining a positive snap judgment. This will then make the homeowner view your knocking as a situational attribute that's worth their attention.

So, how do you go about flipping this within the first few seconds? It all starts with your non-verbal communication.

CHAPTER 5:

THE MAJORITY OF YOUR PITCH HAS NOTHING TO DO WITH WORD CHOICE

Have you ever had someone look you up and down, make an utterly disgusted facial expression, and then slam their door in your face? I have, but you can learn how to decrease the quantity of these ego-deflating encounters.

When you imagine a 'No Soliciting' sign, you probably picture a stick figure holding a briefcase and maybe wearing a tie or nice clothing. Original traveling sales-people typically wore business attire when they showed up unannounced.

Obviously, you want to look presentable, but from my experience, you don't want to overdo it. This can be an obvious sign that you're just another cliché sales person.

It's best to dress the part of what you're selling or who you're portraying yourself as being, which hopefully, is not a solicitor!

In door-to-door sales for example, you typically don't want to combine all of the following: buttoning your polo all the way up, tucking in your polo, slicking your hair, being completely clean-shaven and wearing shorts. Although some successful reps dress in this combination, it did not work well for me at all.

I'm not saying that you shouldn't do what's natural and comfortable for you, but when these are *all combined,* it brings a certain 'solicitation' look to it. You're dressing like a solicitor, which is exactly what you don't want people to categorize you as.

Think about it from a homeowner's perspective – if you were at home and some young, clean cut, well-dressed person knocked on your door, you would not think to yourself, 'I wonder what this sharp-looking fellow is up to.' Realistically, you're more inclined to think, 'Who the hell does this too-good-to-be-true solicitor think they are?'

I'm not saying to dress sloppy or unprofessional, but you need to be mindful that every single detail is going to matter in the first moments leading up to the homeowner permanently judging you. Every detail will be magnified as they decide if you're worth talking to.

For example, when I sold a pest control service door-to-door, I wanted to look more like a service technician than a clean cut young salesman. I would call myself "the bug guy" while dressed more as if I was performing the service rather than just selling it.

This doesn't mean that I dressed *exactly* like a technician; it just means that I wore my uniform more casual. I wore a hat, I allowed myself to have stubble or a short beard and I untucked my shirt; I always wore pants because I never saw a service technician wearing shorts.

What you're wearing and how you're wearing it will almost always be the first piece of evidence that you can use to begin disproving the homeowner's existing event schema.

Start by dressing the part of what you're selling in any way that you can. Don't overdo the idea that you need to look as sharp and as clean cut as possible.

The thing to remember is that people have a strong 'bullshit detector' when you're on their doorstep. They are automatically going to assume that you're selling something (which you are), therefore, you want to do your best to embody something other than just a solicitor.

Getting them to qualify you as a manager or a laborer rather than just a salesperson is a vital piece of evidence that can help you disarm the homeowner's event schema. It's the first step in getting them to assess your arrival as something external and situational rather than internal and flawed.

Your Body Sets the Tone

Screaming is never a good sign, especially not on a full moon at a psychiatric hospital. The patient stood rigidly with her fists at her sides, and her body squared off with the nurse who she was towering over.

The staff member who responded only made the situation worse. He practically mirrored the patient's rigid body language, facing her directly as he attempted to talk her down. The patient began yelling louder, cussing more and threatening severely. This was the point when she usually became violent.

Other staff members were starting to notice the commotion. They began inching closer and closer with concerned looks on their faces. The patient, feeling threatened, looked from one staff member to the next until she saw me.

She knew that I was the shift lead, but I was also the only person who was sitting down. I sat on the arm of a chair with my body turned at a 45-degree angle, trying to look as relaxed as possible.

"What happened?" I asked.

She vented about her medication being denied again. Her yelling and cussing slowly decreased the more that she talked, and the nurse was able to take a few steps back now that the patient's attention was elsewhere.

After a couple validations, she was calm enough to have a conversation and to consider other perspectives of the situation.

Body language is the bulk sum of how we as humans communicate. *What* we say and *how* we say it are important too, but our body language says more than any other form of communication.

If you didn't already know, selling is a transfer of energy.

Your body language plays a huge part in the energy that you transfer. It's important for portraying confidence, positivity, and an overall relaxed nature.

Picture yourself as the homeowner again - you open your front door to a well-dressed stranger who is squared off with you, looking directly into your eyes, and wearing a huge smile. At this point, your event schema is practically solidified. Nothing is going to silence the solicitor alarm blaring in your head.

If your team leader or coach is training you correctly, they'll force you to practice implementing good body language. The good news is that it's fairly easy to understand. The first thing that you want to do is make the homeowner engage with you *before you engage with them.*

You want to make yourself look busy (looking down at your iPad, notes, clipboard, etc.), so that the homeowner speaks first.

Even though you're on their doorstep, you want to confidently send the message that they're stepping into your 'office.' This helps you take immediate control of the interaction.

Being distracted will signal to them that you're working, and that the 'work' you're doing is important enough to have your attention. This act of not being overly eager to engage first will be another piece of evidence to disprove the homeowner's event schema.

Them engaging first is kind of like consent to have a back and forth interaction - you knock, they open their door, they engage, so you engage back. Your distractedness and your body language will likely build curiosity in the homeowner. Making them engage first will create some of the needed push-pull tension.

This is counter-intuitive to how most homeowners think a solicitor would act. They expect you to be overwhelming, cheesy and/or fake.

This is why you don't want to jump down their throat or overwhelm them with fake positive energy. From their point of view, there's no reason (yet) for you to be acting overly excited or eager about this interaction.

We've all had experiences with overwhelming people - or sometimes, you were the overwhelming one - who didn't understand the dynamic of 'push-pull,' mutual engagement, and how to build tension by not trying too hard. It's usually a lesson that we learn at a young age, and it's an important lesson to remember on the doors.

Posture

You don't want to have your body squared off and facing the homeowner directly. This can be perceived as confrontational and/or overwhelming.

It's best to stand at a 45-degree angle or to be completely shouldered off with them. This was a common practice at the psychiatric hospital, and probably something that you naturally do at times already.

You want to appear casual, like you have 'one foot in and one foot out' of the conversation so that you don't seem too overwhelming.

There's a reason that the term 'squaring off' is used to describe two people who look like they're about to fight. Understanding this is very important during initial interactions with homeowners.

Squaring off can make you seem desperate and biased. This will repel homeowners more often than not.

Shouldering off, however, makes you seem more relaxed and neutral.

You need to start off as calm and as non-threatening as possible. Remember to think of your introduction as a de-escalation just as much as a hook to grab their interest. You're a stranger interrupting people in the comfort of their home, so don't give them a shred of evidence that would make them even more eager to get rid of you.

Relaxing and opening up your posture is often what disarms homeowners. It also invites them to perceive this as a neighborhood thing - as you point to the houses of neighbors who are customers - rather than just an individual solicitation.

As for smiling and eye contact, don't overdo it. And don't smile before you've made eye contact with the homeowner.

Wait until they say something to you before you look up, make eye contact and smile. Don't do this in any other order, and don't think that you need to force yourself to wear a huge smile. Just smile as subtly or as naturally as you can so that you don't wear the face of a stereotypical solicitor.

Later on in the sale, you can definitely incorporate big smiles whenever natural circumstances arise. Remember that selling is a transfer of energy, but you want to make sure that it's authentic energy rather than fake.

Personally, I didn't smile much during initial eye contact because it looked forced and fake, but I definitely smiled big whenever it felt natural. Homeowners can almost always tell the difference.

The Habits You Need to Eliminate

It's extremely easy to form bad habits with body language. How frequently do we have to remind ourselves to not slouch our posture while we're seated?

In regards to body language, the most typical bad habits include, shifting your weight back and forth, talking with your hands too much and bobbing your head excessively (I'm referring to the 'bobble head' type of movement). These habits signal nervousness and a lack of confidence, whether we're actually nervous or not.

You want to appear calm and confident in order to continue to stack evidence against the other person's event schema.

Here's what I recommend:

1) If you find yourself shifting your weight back and forth too much, then put all of your weight on one foot. Staying firmly planted will have a subconscious effect on the homeowner's perspective of your comfortability and confidence.

2) If you struggle with moving your hands too much, put your free hand on your hip and keep an object in your other hand (iPad, pen, etc.). You can also plan times to purposefully point at things and draw the homeowner's attention.

   For example, you can point at the homes of neighbors who are current customers. Or if you're selling pest control, you can point to parts of the homeowner's house as you talk about details of the service. This gives your hand movements purpose, and it also allows for times to break eye contact and draw their attention elsewhere.

3) If you struggle with being a 'bobble head,' practice nodding your head up and down when you talk (not side to side or circularly at all).

Nodding (and smiling) is very powerful while talking and also while listening.

It's another subconscious trick that primes the homeowner into agreement. It raises the odds of them saying 'yes' later on, especially when you start resolving some of their concerns.

Nodding while talking portrays confidence and certainty. It doesn't need to be huge head nods, and you don't need to nod every time you talk, but it should still be implemented more often than not. It will always have a positive effect on the homeowner.

As far as when you're listening, nodding expresses that you're agreeing with them. Even if they're objecting or trying to tell you 'no,' you should always nod and smile. It subconsciously primes them to stay in a constant state of agreement and shows that you're confident and unwavering. It also keeps the door open for negotiation.

You want to stay firm in your confidence and positivity regardless of what you're told. This is required for most sales because you will almost always go through multiple 'nos' or objections before anyone tells you 'yes.'

Positive energy is always your job to generate and then maintain, regardless of what energy the homeowner hits you with. This subconscious transfer of energy is responsible for the majority of sales.

It all starts with your mentality and your confidence to persistently prime the homeowner with positivity. It'll also help a lot when having to challenge and nudge home-owners in the desired direction.

Six Feet

Another thing worth mentioning is that you should stand about six feet away from their door after you knock. You don't want to stand too close because it can make the homeowner uncomfortable or intimidated (especially now during the COVID pandemic), but you also don't want to stand too far away. This can seem impersonal.

Feel free to step a little closer as you begin comfortably conversing though. You can do this by having something in your hand to physically show the homeowner. It seems very natural to take a step or two closer in order to show them something.

Ultimately, your body language should always be relaxed, non-confrontational, confident and purposeful. Implement these tips before you start selling. Body language can make or break a lot of sales.

Mirroring/Matching

One of the most powerful forms of body language is called 'mirroring.' This means that you're simply matching their body language.

If they lean against their door frame or the side of their house, you lean against it as well. If they sit down, you can also sit down. If they smile, you should also smile. If they maintain a more serious demeanor, then you should also maintain a more serious demeanor. The list goes on.

Mirroring someone makes them feel as though you're 'like them,' which gets you closer to their 'in' group.

Just remember to wait a few seconds and be subtle about it instead of obviously copying them.

It's a natural human tendency to mirror those who we like. You probably do it subconsciously with friends and family members, but it's easily forgotten during sales interactions when you're trying to think about your own body language as well as what you're supposed to say.

This is why it's important to have thoroughly practiced and prepared before knocking. You want to save as much of your cognitive attention as possible for the homeowner's body language and responses during the conversation.

Pro tip – you can even implement your own body language that you want *them* to mirror. Remember, every move that you make should be purposeful. When you know that the homeowner is curious and engaged, you can start being the first one to lean against the house or sit down because the other person will likely start to mirror *you*.

There is a scene in the 2010 The Karate Kid movie where Mr. Han takes Dre (Jayden Smith) up to a temple in the mountains. When they get to the temple, Dre notices a woman and a snake facing each other and copying each other's movements. Dre then asks Mr. Han why the woman is copying the snake, but Mr. Han corrects Dre. Mr. Han points out that the snake is actually the one copying the woman.

The point I'm trying to make is that mirroring goes both ways. Mirroring the other person is very effective, but you'll find that homeowners will mirror you as well if you've generated interest and a positive snap judgment.

Implementing body language that you want the other person to mirror is one of the best ways to take control of a sale.

One of the best tricks that I ever learned was utilizing the sitting position. If you can get yourself and the other person to both sit down, I guarantee that it will raise your odds of closing the deal. People are much more willing to make deals while sitting down. It's much more relaxed, friendly and negotiable; it also works as a micro commitment to gauge their interest level.

If they seem engaged and interested, you can then ask if you can sit down (as long as you feel comfortable doing so). This is not a requirement, and not something that you need to do every time; it's just something that can work extremely well whenever you feel the opportunity arise.

When you're both sitting down, it's much harder for the homeowner to get rid of you by saying 'no.' Sitting down signals that you're staying put. It will be a pathway that leads you right into productive sales dialogue.

Sitting down gets you closer to the 'guest' category rather than the 'stranger' or 'solicitor' category, and ultimately gets you closer to the other person's 'in' group.

A trick that I learned was to simply ask, "my legs are killing me from being on them all day, do you mind if we sit down?" If you can tell from the beginning that they are interested, this can be a great strategy to use. They will almost always say yes, and if they're interested, they will be more willing to consider your offer.

Homeowners are more likely to consider buying when you create a relaxed and positive environment.

Getting the homeowner to mirror your enthusiasm and positivity is extremely powerful as well. Smiling, head nodding, laughing, and engaging with them (like you would a close friend) will go a very long way.

When they speak, make them feel like you enjoy listening to what they have to say. Oftentimes, they will reciprocate this and then take more interest in your offer.

Although your positivity and enthusiasm need to seem natural instead of forced, you will greatly benefit from learning how to generate this transfer of energy on cue. After your introduction, when you've generated a mutual conversation, you can easily display this energy without it seeming fake or forced. This is one of the quickest rapport-building tools that will transition you into more sales dialogue.

CHAPTER 6:
HOW TO BREAK THE CAMEL'S BACK

Red and blue lights flash in your rearview mirror as you're driving. You feel your heart rate freeze and then start climbing. You pull over and see the police officer exit his vehicle and walk towards you. You open your window as he approaches. "License and registration, please," he says.

When you imagine the officer saying the word 'please,' how do you imagine him saying it? Does his tone of voice go up or does it go down? It goes down, obviously. There's no uncertainty in his voice, as he is not asking; he is telling.

Confidence/certainty ends with a down tone, whereas questioning/uncertainty ends with an up tone.

Our tone, volume, pitch and speed are referred to as 'paraverbal' communication. Paraverbal communication is *how* we say the words that we're saying, and it accounts for almost 40% of our overall communication. Paraverbals can make or break a sale just like body language.

We've all listened to robots and automated voices. Although, with time, they will get better, they're usually flat, boring and unchanging. Talking like this will make it obvious to homeowners that you're rote-rehearsing a script. You'll sound like a broken record that's been played all over the neighborhood.

Strong paraverbal communication will help you portray uniqueness and confidence, and it will provide scarcity to the initial discount in your introduction. You must implement your paraverbals so convincingly that the words 'script' or 'pitch' never cross the homeowner's mind.

Failure to do so can easily reinforce their belief in you being a stereotypical solicitor.

Unless you're asking a question, using an up tone will often give your control away to the homeowner. Down tones maintain confidence and certainty (just like how authority figures speak). This is really important to remember during the introduction, and especially when you're closing.

Most people accidentally use up tones at the end of their sentences. This is what you need to be very mindful of. People will perceive you as having less confidence and less authority if you're ending your sentences with up tones.

A down tone should always be used when making a statement, especially when closing. You need to sound as confident and as certain as possible, so that you also make them feel confident and certain. This will give you a sense of authority and credibility.

When it comes to the speed of which you talk, you don't want to be a motor mouth.

There are times, especially during your introduction, when you want to purposefully slow down. For example, you want to slow down and magnify your discount as much as possible.

When you state the exact discount, or when you use phrases like 'half-off' and 'group rate,' you need to slow down, slightly lower the volume of your voice, and use a down tone. This paraverbal combination will magnify the importance and the scarcity of the discount.

The good news is that you can perfect the paraverbals in your introduction before you even start knocking. Since your introduction should be the exact same almost every single time, having a strong delivery should already be engrained into you and perfected.

However, it's easy to start speaking too quickly after your introduction. You get nervous or eager to get through your pitch. Remember to slow down and pause before responding. Digest what they tell you. Remind yourself that the confidence that you portray through your paraverbals is just as important as the words you actually say.

As for the volume of your voice, it should vary throughout different points in the sale. The general

rule, however, is that it's better to talk loudly than to talk quietly.

This obviously doesn't mean that you should yell, it just means that you want to sound confident and enthusiastic when you speak. Failure to do so can create hesitance and/or a negative qualification from the other person.

Your volume should be a little above average until you share a valuable piece of information - the discount. This is when you want to lower your voice as if you're telling a secret.

Imagine a time when somebody told you a secret or a valuable piece of information. Maybe it was a rumor or some sort of gossip. They knew that they had your full attention as they lowered their voice and you 'perked your ears' in response.

Lowering your voice (as if telling a secret) draws others in. It magnifies the information and signifies the importance of it.

How much you lower your voice doesn't need to be overly obvious; it just needs to be subtle enough for the listener to pick up on, and they will instinctively recognize the discount as valuable information.

Lower your voice, slow down and use a down tone during these important parts. This combination can be stronger than any words that you string together, and the good news is, you can perfectly implement it into your introduction so that it becomes muscle memory.

Remember to utilize strong paraverbals throughout the rest of the sale as well. As you go over your pitch, practice being mindful of these. The last thing you want is for a homeowner to sense a lack of confidence and certainty in your voice.

CHAPTER 7:
"HI MY NAME IS (BULLSHIT), AND I AM WITH (BULLSHIT)"

This is what most homeowners actually hear whenever solicitors use this cliché introduction. Homeowners could not care any less about what your name is (yet) and what company you're representing (yet), until they at least know what you're selling or what you're doing.

As long as you've nailed your non-verbal communication, this is when *what* you say becomes important as well. Immediately introducing your name and the name of your company is great in many lines of sales, but it's not nearly as beneficial in door-to-door sales.

This is because it *sounds* like the intro to a sales encounter. It confirms the event schema of the homeowner and makes their snap judgment work against you, pushing you further into their 'out' group or 'solicitor' category.

In door-to-door sales, introducing your name and the name of your company is counterproductive and a waste of time (during your introduction).

Remember that you only have a few seconds to attain a positive snap judgment. If you waste time introducing your name and your company – or talking about the team flag hanging above their garage door that just so happens to be your 'favorite team' as well – then you will usually reinforce the homeowner's negative event schema. This happens for two reasons.

First, the homeowner has heard this exact intro from sales reps in the past. It's cliché and it's typical for a solicitor/sales person to say. Second, the homeowner still has no idea why you're there (which is the only thing that they care about at first).

They want to know what you're doing or what you're selling before they will care to know anything else. If you waste their time with information that they don't care about, you will dig yourself into a deeper hole of a stereotypical solicitor.

Remember that snap judgments happen in a matter of seconds.

You need to cut the fat out of your introduction, and only keep what works as evidence against the homeowner's event schema.

Wasting time will keep you further away from their 'in' group, and make you seem 'just like all the other solicitors.'

Unfortunately, most companies that do door-to-door sales have this introduction implemented into their sales script. Although there are some successful reps that use this intro, from personal experience, I can say that it didn't work well for me. You haven't earned the right to be on a first name basis yet.

The effective - and respectful - thing to do is to not waste anyone's time. You want to get right to the point and address the 'elephant in the room.' This shows empathy, which is the next piece of evidence to stack against the homeowner's event schema.

"The reason I'm here..."

In general, you have a couple options regarding the first thing that you say. You can ask, "how are you?" "how's it going?" or "are you the boss?" If the first two options feel fake or awkward, then go with, "are you the boss?" This third option can help you qualify the person as being the 'decision-maker' of the household.

It also doesn't sound as fake or cliché as "how are you?" and "how's it going?" Instead, "are you the boss?" gets right to the point. It doesn't beat around the bush or sound like a cheesy rapport-building question.

There are situations, however, that allow you to deviate from one of these typical openings. For example:

1) The homeowner opens their door and a barking dog(s) greets you.

   It can be natural and sometimes funny to say something like, "You have a good guard dog," especially if the dog is of a smaller breed. This usually gets the homeowner to laugh or relax a little bit. Everyone loves their dogs, so quickly address this and then dive right into your introduction.

2) The homeowner immediately asks, "What are you selling?"

   To this, I always responded with, "Well, what are you buying?" This almost always gets a laugh and makes light of the question. Then you can quickly move on to the reason you're there.

After this quick first part, you want to start your introduction with "the reason I'm here..." and then get right to the point.

In other words, tell them who you are without telling them your name or the name of your company. "The reason I'm here" is the closest thing to 'magic words' that I ever came across when knocking. It lets the homeowner know that you're getting right to the point without wasting any time.

This is the most empathetic thing that you can do, and it also helps you to quickly qualify the potential buyers from the non-buyers. I'll talk more about this part later.

Here's an example of how my pest control introduction would start: The homeowner opens their door and engages first. I look up and ask one of the three intro questions. The homeowner answers the question, and then I respond with, "The reason I'm here, I'm the bug guy for (insert names of neighbors) …"

There's no need to beat around the bush here. 'The reason I'm here' will help to neutralize their immediate impression of you, since it quickly answers the only question that they currently care about. This will help you be perceived as professional and courteous since you're asking for the homeowner's time.

So now that they know the answer to their only question, it allows you to qualify their reaction and decide the next step.

Getting right to the point will be *another* piece of evidence that helps you disarm the homeowner's event schema.

When combined correctly, your body language, paraverbal communication, and word choice will raise your odds of being perceived as an authority figure, just as I explained in the section titled 'paraverbals.'

Starting in 1961, social psychologist Stanley Milgram conducted a study titled 'Obedience to Authority.' The study helped explain the power that an authority figure can have on people.

In summary, Milgram found that participants would willingly obey a perceived authority figure to the extent of sending extremely painful shock waves to a person who was under interrogation. Knowingly to the participants, the shock waves gradually increased in strength to the point of lethal intensity.

Obviously, no one was actually being shocked, but the participants didn't know that. The participants thought that there really was a person in the other room being interrogated because of the screams that they would hear.

The participants were told by a perceived authority figure to sit down and administer the shock waves when instructed. This included raising the intensity after each shock. In one instance, a participant sent strong enough shock waves to kill the person being interrogated.

Regardless of the distress that participants felt from administering the pain, they remained obedient to the perceived authority figure for a lot longer than predicted.

This study had obvious ethical concerns and would have never been allowed in modern experiments, but it goes to show the influence that a perceived authority figure can have on a person.

Milgram's study helped explain some of the psychology behind Nazi prison guards, and what could have made them continue to obey such horrendous orders during

WW2. Other than prejudice and brainwashing, it had a lot to do with obedience to authority.

When selling door-to-door, you want to be perceived as an authority figure (or as close to it as possible), and perfecting your introduction is a good way to do that.

Whether or not the homeowner buys, they will be much more willing to have a conversation and respect you in the first place. This means that they have perceived you as being professional, confident and respectable.

Think of it this way - when you go to see a doctor or a physical therapist, they will tell you what they highly recommend you do. Are you going to do what they recommend? Well, whether you do it or not, the point is that you will listen to them and respect their recommendation.

Later on, I'll share more ways to raise your odds of being perceived as an authority figure, but for now, let's come back to your name and the name of your company.

The best thing to do is to delay telling the homeowner your name until the conversation gets going. Wait until later on in the sale - once the homeowner is actually conversing - to offer your name. This is more of a natural and personable time to do so.

Once you've given sufficient evidence to disprove their event schema, offering your name will seem more genuine. This will not seem 'fake' or like a waste of time anymore because they've welcomed the conversation. Offering your name now is sort of a pleasantry and a 'how silly of me' moment that is typically perceived positively.

It's also very powerful to offer a handshake when introducing your name because it creates a stronger connection. Physical touch can release a neurochemical called 'oxytocin.' Oxytocin is associated with feelings of empathy, trust and relationship building.

This is why it's important to create a positive snap judgment and then get them engaged in a conversation. Only then can you introduce your name and give them a physical handshake.

Oxytocin is a key neurochemical that when activated, will greatly increase your likelihood of connecting with someone and influencing them. Although shaking hands is very discouraged these days because of COVID, I promise that the vast majority of people won't care after you've been conversing.

This is not a political stance. This is just based on my experience of knocking doors in Portland, OR during the heart of the pandemic. As long as you initially maintain a good social distance, then you will usually find that people warm up quickly and don't fear a handshake.

We as humans are social animals and have an innate need to engage with others and feel connected. This understanding can be heavily used to your advantage.

These days, people have been forced to spend more time alone than ever before (or at least just out of the community). More people are isolated and/or working from home, and this has naturally caused a craving for more human connection.

So here's the order of operations: make your intro quick and to the point, ask a question and allow the conversation to build, then say "my name is (insert name) by the way," and hold out your hand.

In most other lines of sales, you will usually introduce yourself and shake hands at the very beginning, but you want to delay this in door-to-door sales because homeowners have no obligation to be respectful towards you at first. You need to be qualified positively before they will care to know your name or even consider shaking your hand.

As for the name of your company, I found that it was usually better to have the homeowner specifically ask for it later on. If you do everything correctly to control their snap judgment, then introducing the name of your company doesn't matter as much as you might think.

When you hold back this information, it will even make the homeowner think of *you* more than they would think of a big over-arching company. A good sign is when a homeowner asks if you're the owner of the company. This sense of ownership and authority is very powerful and very beneficial.

When you're talking, you should always be saying 'I,' 'me,' and 'my company' rather than 'us,' 'we,' and 'our company.'

This is because you want to show a sense of ownership. This small change will make the homeowner perceive you as an authority figure even more.

Mirroring/Matching (Again)

One day at the psychiatric hospital, I was outside with the same patient who I'd had to restrain into a security car. He had been playing soccer with some of the other patients before becoming angry with one of them. Instead of retaliating, though, he decided to walk away.

As we walked, he kept responding with "fuck you" to everything that I said, and as we got closer to the building, he started walking in a different direction. When I tried redirecting him, he unsurprisingly replied, "fuck you," and kept walking away.

Chasing or redirecting him would have made the situation worse (as we'd learned the hard way), so instead, I just sat down and told him to let me know when he was ready to go inside.

He paced around, punted a basketball and acted like he was going to walk out of sight (while glancing back to see my reaction), but I didn't budge. He eventually gave up and started walking back towards the building, and as he walked past me, he said, "fuck you."

When we got back inside, I walked him to his bedroom and unlocked his door. As I turned to leave, he asked me, "Can you get me some tea from the kitchen?"

I kept walking as I looked back and replied, "No, because fuck me, right?"

To this, he smirked, and calmly went into his room without a problem. I was one of the only staff who built solid rapport with him because the only way to do that was to match him at his level and speak his language.

Matching and mirroring others goes deeper than just body language.

Imagine a spectrum. On one end of the spectrum is a homeowner who answers the door smiling and who happily engages with you. They show no signs of skepticism or annoyance. On the other end of the spectrum, however, is a homeowner who answers the door with a scowl or a very serious look. They'll ask something passive aggressive like "what are you selling?" or "can I help you?" or "did you not see my 'no soliciting' sign?"

Homeowners will almost always fall somewhere on the spectrum between these two examples. Counterintuitively, though, it doesn't matter where they fall. There's always a chance to sell them regardless of their initial demeanor. I can't say for certain any 'perfect' demeanor that I would hope to encounter.

Every homeowner is different regardless of whether they're a potential buyer or not, and you will miss out on a lot of sales if you're intimidated by certain types of people.

Always be confident and 'assume the sale' until you've gathered factual evidence to disprove this.

So, how do you effectively match and mirror the other person's demeanor within the first few seconds? It starts with their reaction to you asking, "how are you?" or "how's it going?" or "are you the boss?"

Their reaction should give you a good understanding of where they fall. This will help you judge how quick/slow and happy/serious you should be. Do they seem happy/annoyed? Do they seem like they're in a hurry? Do they seem relaxed or like they have all the time in the world? Do they step onto the porch and close the door behind them? Do they just peek their head through the crack in the door?

This will determine how much you smile, how quickly you should get to the point, how tentative you should be and how far or how close you should stand to them.

Their demeanor and overall 'vibe' should be matched and catered to. This displays empathy and similarity that will help with the homeowner's snap judgment of you.

The best practice is to assume that everybody will be initially short with you and/or passive aggressive. Assume that you will need to get right to the point without getting too caught up in smiling and all of the pleasantries. Let it be a pleasant surprise whenever somebody is pleasant with you.

Just remember to *cater* to the person you're talking to, and expect them to be a little bit skeptical at first. Get right to the point and act 'like them' so that you can continue stacking evidence against their event schema.

CHAPTER 8:

HOW TO HANDLE A KAREN

E veryone lies. Studies have suggested that around 60% of people will lie at least once in just a ten-minute conversation.

How good of a liar are you? How good are you at bluffing without giving yourself away? I ask you this because you need to be a good liar when selling door-to-door. You need to be a good actor.

I'm not saying that you're ever going to blatantly lie; hopefully, you don't ever blatantly lie to a homeowner.

What I'm saying is that most people will try to negatively qualify you as a solicitor. Therefore, it's your job to subconsciously convince them that you're not.

The better you convince yourself of the lie being the truth, the better you will be able to convince others as well. The more deeply you believe that you're not a solicitor, the better you'll be at making others believe it too.

When you encounter a Karen (or whatever the male name of this is called), they will feed off of your inability to keep composure. If you mess up and give them evidence that reinforces their initial event schema, sometimes, they will double down on their anger and let it out on you.

Think back to the section on mentality. How well have you convinced yourself that you're of genuine benefit to the neighborhood? How well have you convinced yourself that you're absolutely *not* a solicitor? This will show when you encounter a Karen.

If you shuffle your feet, widen your eyes, stutter or have a shaky voice, then you probably haven't convinced yourself well enough yet. If somebody is ever blatantly angry and disrespectful, you can confidently apologize and walk away.

But nobody should ever have the power to take away your confidence or composure. Rather, you need to learn how to positively challenge their perspective.

What's important to understand is that stereotypical solicitors all present themselves in ways that reinforce home-owners' event schemas. They dive into a canned pitch, and then lose composure when they run into a Karen. Then they walk away and move onto the next house, the next neighborhood, or perhaps even the next job.

This is exactly how Karens and other skeptical home-owners *expect you to act;* so, by choosing to maintain your confidence and your composure, you are actively disproving their event schema. It then leaves you room to generate a sense of credibility by referencing yourself to a nearby neighbor that's a customer.

Confidence, composure and credibility will often make the homeowner qualify you as unique (unlike how solicitors probably responded to their outbursts in the past), and make them feel bad about their outburst.

If you're truly convinced that you're not a solicitor, then you won't act like one. Every single ounce of your communication will portray this belief, and work as a last-ditch effort to flip the homeowner's snap judgment.

If you're able to break free from a Karen's 'stereotypical solicitor' snap judgment, then you will likely remain in their good graces for the rest of the interaction. You can then leverage this if they end up having an interest or a need for what you're selling.

Remember that your composure and credibility can oftentimes be a de-escalation. A Karen will often need you to 'speak their language' in a way that's not disrespectful.

Indirectly challenging their perspective will sometimes catch them off guard, and once they know that you're a 'friend of a friend' in regards to their neighbors, then you're practically in the clear. Here's a sample response:

"Give me the boot anytime, but I actually take care of your neighbor, Cobi. I'm his bug guy. A lot of the neighbors have been getting ants really bad recently. How are you doing with the bug situation?"

However, remember the sales funnel; this will not work every time (it will likely fail more often than not). But ultimately, it will work multiple times per day, and of those times, there can often be a couple potential buyers.

Cognitive Dissonance

Shredded schoolwork was scattered around the patient's feet. The shouting and cussing kept getting louder, especially when he was brought new copies of the schoolwork and told that he was required to complete it.

Unfortunately for me, I was the patient's primary staff member for the next shift. I had to find a way to manage his outbursts while also maintaining the same expectation about completing the schoolwork. Before approaching him, I got a cup of water from the kitchen and brought it to his room.

Immediately after opening his door, I became the new target for his anger. He let me know, loud and clear, that no schoolwork was going to be done. I stood calmly in the doorway and nodded along with what he was yelling until he finally stopped.

"Hey man, I'm just here to bring you some water. I'm your primary for this shift. Your throat must be sore."

"Oh, sorry," he said before chugging the whole cup.

"What's making you not want to finish your work?" I asked.

By the end of our conversation, we had compromised on him doing half of his schoolwork. But later, when I came over to collect it, he had completed everything other than one part that he didn't understand.

'Cognitive dissonance' can be a powerful tool to use whenever somebody has an incorrect snap judgment of you. It's defined as a state of cognitive displeasure that occurs when having a direct experience that actively opposes a core belief, thus inciting a change in behavior.

Let's assume someone is smoking a cigarette on their front porch when their sibling and nephew pull into the driveway. The person believes that smoking is bad, and they don't want their nephew to see them smoking. Therefore, they put out the cigarette and toss it out of sight.

Here's another example. The mailman walks up to a person's house and knocks on the door, and the homeowner comes out screaming at the mailman about how much they hate solicitors, only to find out that the person is just delivering a package. This makes the homeowner feel bad about their outburst and then immediately apologize for their mistake.

In relation to door-to-door sales, the homeowner believes that they're respectful to other respectable people. So, they're much more likely to treat you with respect if they qualify you positively (especially if they were initially disrespectful).

Controlling and flipping snap judgments will make homeowners much more willing to have a conversation with you. The homeowner will begin to perceive you uniquely rather than as a stereotypical solicitor.

This is often the knockout punch (the final piece of evidence) to disprove their event schema, and will be what gets your foot in the door in order to progress into real sales dialogue.

Be Respectful

One last obvious thing to mention – you should never be disrespectful. Getting yelled at, cussed at or harassed can unfortunately be part of the job, and homeowners will rarely empathize with the difficult work that you're doing.

Someone may unleash their anger on you when you're having one of your hardest days, and you will have to hold back from retaliating or letting it negatively affect your cognitive triangle.

All that you can do is minimize the quantity and intensity of these interactions by preparing for them in advance. Understand that attaining a positive snap judgment is often dependent on de-escalation, and sometimes, the best de-escalation tactic is to confidently utilize cognitive dissonance.

Challenging somebody who is skeptical or annoyed can be disarming and beneficial to your first impression, but if a person is ever continuously angry or disrespectful towards you, then just apologize and walk away. If there's no hope in flipping their snap judgment after your first attempt, don't waste your time and don't give room for the situation to get worse.

CHAPTER 9:
SEEING THROUGH SMOKESCREENS

A re you a liar? How many times have you lied in order to not hurt another person's feelings? Maybe you've used the cliché breakup line, 'It's not you, it's me.'

Lying can be necessary, and you'll find that homeowners lie to you all the time. A lot of them would rather 'let you down' as softly as possible than blatantly tell you 'no.' Assuming that you've successfully manipulated their snap judgment, it's still common that they'll want to end the interaction.

This doesn't mean that they don't like you or that they're not interested in your offer. It's usually just because they're not interested *enough* to commit to the conversation, or their event schema is still telling them to get out as quickly and as easily as possible.

Committing to the conversation means that they'll have to trust you enough to put cognitive effort into considering your offer. Then they'll either have to buy, or they'll have to let you down harder than they would have if they'd just lied to you in the first place.

Oftentimes, homeowners will try to end the interaction right after your introduction, regardless of how well you've controlled their snap judgment of you. They won't be very willing to commit to sales dialogue.

This is when you need to stay in control of the conversation. You need to push the conversation along in order to create a mutual interaction.

The way that homeowners lie to you after your introduction is by giving you a 'smokescreen.' The only intention of a smokescreen is to get you to leave as quickly and as gently as possible. This is because most people don't like conflict.

Instead of saying 'no,' they'd rather tell you that they're 'in a hurry' so it's not a good time. They'd rather tell you to 'leave a card' so that they can call you when they need you, or tell you that their spouse 'is the one to talk to' (but that their spouse isn't home or able to be reached by phone).

The most important thing to remember is that these people can be the *easiest* to sell if you're just willing to push past their initial smokescreen(s).

Never let a smokescreen stunt the direction of the conversation. Address it slightly, and then quickly move on. Get it into your head now that quick objections are usually lies, unless it's later on in the sale (which I'll get to later).

Respond to smokescreens as though you've heard each one a thousand times. Convince yourself that smokescreens hold no weight. This keeps you in control of the conversation, and gives you more time to build rapport and interest. This will transition you into the sales dialogue that will disclose their likelihood of buying.

So what do you do about smokescreens? Let's start with the things that you do *not* do.

You do not linger on them. What I mean by this is that you want to move the conversation along as quickly and as seamlessly as possible.

Imagine how a sprinter jumps over hurdles during a race – they barely get slowed down at all, and they rarely ever trip. Smokescreens shouldn't slow you down or trip you up because they're rarely based in truth. The only truth is that the homeowner is lying in order to avoid the situation entirely.

You want to quickly address smokescreens but then disregard them and move on. Here are some examples that you should play around with.

When they say that they're in a hurry, tell them, "no worries, this will be really quick," and then move on.

When they ask you to leave your business card, tell them that you would if you could, "but unfortunately, it's not a call-in discount," and then move on.

When they say that their spouse is the one to talk to then ask them, "awesome, will you go get him/her, so we can all talk?" or "awesome, let's call them; what's their number?" If they're adamant that they cannot make a decision alone, ask them when their spouse will be home so that you can come back.

One way to think of this is that you're trying to back the homeowner into a corner where they have to disclose the truth. Getting told, "No, I do not want your service," is better to be done sooner rather than later. If they tell you 'no' outright, then it speeds up your buyer qualification process.

However, you will find that backing homeowners into a conversational corner will make a lot of them more willing to consider your offer. They'll be more open to authentic sales dialogue because you're kind of forcing it out of them.

You're nudging them in the direction that they aren't willing to nudge themselves in.

Think of this whole process as if you're saying to the homeowner, 'I can see through the bullshit that you're feeding me, so I'm going to move this conversation along and get to the truth one way or another.'

Just because they give a smokescreen doesn't mean that they're not interested. Sometimes, they have a strong need or want for what you're offering, but you haven't had enough time to build up the required trust and rapport. They don't yet feel comfortable disclosing their interest level.

This is why you need to push the conversation along and give yourself more time to create the trust and rapport that's required for a door-to-door sale.

Pushing past a smokescreen keeps you in control and puts you in a place of authority as you guide them into authentic sales dialogue. Any homeowner who is genuinely interested will likely respect you a little bit and allow for more of a rapport-building process.

Obviously, however, there will be times when their initial smokescreen is based on the truth. You will inevitably run into instances where they really are in a hurry or they really do need to you come back and talk to their spouse.

It's still important to push through these initial smokescreens so that you can discover this truth and then decide the best route forward (Should you call their bluff? Should you come back later? Should you not come back?).

In most lines of sales, potential customers are going to use smokescreens. Once you've been in sales for long enough, you will have heard the same smokescreens over and over, and will rarely get surprised by something new. This makes pushing past them a lot easier because you naturally form a 'tried and true' response to just about every single one.

However, it is important to remember the sales funnel – quickly moving past smokescreens is not foolproof. It will likely fail as much as it succeeds. But then again, the purpose of doing this is so that you push a lot more potential buyers into real sales dialogue. This way, you can build the necessary trust and rapport as well as disclose the truth about their likelihood of buying. This will inevitably make you more sales compared to walking away every time you're hit with a smokescreen.

Lastly, make sure that you never appear flustered or upset when hit with a smokescreen.

You must never let them affect your appearance or demeanor in any way (other than nodding your head and smiling). Don't ever appear negatively affected.

Instead, act as if you've heard this same thing a thousand times already. The easiest way to portray this message to the homeowner is by smiling and nodding your head, so, practice this regardless of what is said to you.

Remember that your cognitive triangle will affect your body language and inevitably determine your ability to make more sales. The ability to confidently and positively push through smokescreens is a 'light bulb moment' that will propel you into a higher rank of success.

CHAPTER 10:

THE ONLY MATH YOU NEED TO KNOW

When you were a kid, weren't you thrilled every time you were given math homework, especially in high school when it looked more like a foreign language? You were probably as thrilled as my old psychiatric patient who ripped his up.

Fortunately for you, there's no math homework for door-to-door selling. There's only the appreciation for the rational truth that numbers will provide you.

Unlike homeowners, the numbers won't lie. The numbers clearly show that you will run into far more non-buyers than buyers (regardless of how well the other person snap judges you). Therefore, your goal is to qualify the non-buyers as quickly as possible so that you can move on to the next house.

Quickly parting ways with somebody who is a hard 'no' is a victory. There are no magic words to turn them into a 'yes.' The only failure here is if you waste too much time with them.

You will run into rejection far more than you will run into success. Make peace with the inevitability of this! This is why it's important to get right to the point, control the homeowner's snap judgment and judge their level of engagement.

This is part of what you need to prepare your mentality for. Rejection is part of the game, and if you don't make peace with that, you will have a hard time moving on from it (mentally and physically).

In order to qualify the non-buyers from the potential buyers accurately, you need to be willing to push through smokescreens. You need to be able to push at least one time before you'll ever know if they're interested or not.

Regardless of what your closing ratio is, the fact is that you will make more sales by getting yourself in front of more qualified buyers. There are three main failures to learn from: spending too much time with non-buyers, failing to close potential buyers, and letting your cognitive triangle turn negative.

Asking a question at the end of your introduction is the best way to qualify the homeowner's level of interest as quickly as possible.

This tests their willingness to engage with you. Their quality of answer is a great indicator of their current interest level, and is also the most common time for them to give you a smokescreen.

Giving them the opportunity to engage is great for a lot of reasons, even if they give you a smokescreen. This will speed up the qualification process. Either they'll give you a hard 'no' (which allows you to leave and save time) or they'll begin to engage in sales dialogue with you. Either way, the truth is more likely to come out.

When selling pest control, I used to ask, "you're gonna be here in a couple hours, right?" or "what do you do about the bugs?" after my introduction. How much the home-owner elaborated or 'played along' with my question was usually a good predictor of their buying likelihood.

It's worth mentioning, however, that you need to watch out for talkers. There are some people who will talk your ear off with no intention of buying. This is why it's important to keep the conversation focused on sales dia-logue. If the homeowner keeps trying to get off topic, then it's usually best to move on to the next house.

It takes experience to intuitively qualify people quickly, so at first, you want to make sure that you are pushing through 'no's' and smokescreens a couple of times (unless the homeowner is very stern and certainly a 'no'). Ask questions, and be pleasantly persistent until you're abso-lutely certain that they are a non-buyer.

Remember, you cannot turn a hard 'no' into a 'yes.' Your job is to turn 'maybe' into 'yes' with as many qualified buyers as possible.

Time is money when you're on the doors. Remember that it's a 'numbers' game. Wasting even just one extra minute with each non-buyer roughly adds up to a full hour every single day. Good reps can make hundreds of dollars in an hour. Don't let 'nos' slow you down, or worse, *get* you down. They're just part of the game.

Think of it like baseball. You're not going to swing at every pitch that's thrown to you. Of the pitches that you *do* swing at, odds are that it will be an unproductive swing. Even the best professional hitters fail a lot more than they succeed, **but it's the best of the best who never let their last at-bat negatively affect their next one.**

Your goal is to raise your batting average little by little, every single day, and to slowly expand your sales funnel by improving upon your failures, without letting them have a negative effect on you.

CHAPTER 11

HOW TO BUILD INSTANT CREDIBILITY

R eferences are usually the most important part of a re-sume. Other than a degree or diploma, how is an em-ployer supposed to trust you - a stranger - without having anyone who can vouch for your experience, skills, and work ethic?

Reviews work in the exact same way. How are you supposed to spend money on a product or service that doesn't have good reviews? Or any reviews at all?

Better yet, a stranger is just a stranger until you learn that they're friends with somebody who *you* are friends with as well. Then all of a sudden, they become part of your 'in' group.

You're probably thinking that 'you already know' the importance of mentioning nearby neighbors who are cus-tomers. It's likely already implemented into your script, as it should be, so I'm not going to elaborate too deeply.

Instead, I'm going to explain some of the psychology and alternative methods to name-dropping neighbors.

Referencing neighbors is for your own credibility. It's one of the strongest pieces of evidence to flip a homeowner's event schema.

Regardless of their level of interest, you will often disarm their skepticism and see an instant change in their demeanor. They'll be more willing to trust you because you've given yourself a sense of belonging.

For example, "The reason I'm here is, I'm the bug guy for John, Jane and Cobi from two houses down..." Notice how this is stripped of useless information. It quickly and effectively covers the only information that the homeowner currently cares to know (who you are and whether you're worth listening to).

Pro tip – If you're going to mention multiple neighbors, then use the name of the closest neighbor *last*.

The homeowner might not know the first two names that you drop, but they will instantly believe you if they *do know* the name of the last neighbor you mention.

This partly has to do with something called the 'recency effect.' The recency effect explains that when multiple pieces of information are given, humans will more clearly remember the final piece of information.

So, if a homeowner has a very close neighbor who is a customer of yours, make sure to mention that name last.

This final piece of credible information will build momentum into the next part of your introduction.

Effective name-dropping can also trigger social conformity. Some homeowners will become very curious if they know that their neighbors use you and trust you. This will open the door for authentic sales dialogue and make your job a whole lot easier. You will effectively set yourself up to be as persuasive as possible.

As you dive into sales dialogue, it's important that you continue to mention neighbors. Potential buyers do not want to hear you talk about why *they* should buy; they want to hear you talk about why *their neighbor(s)* bought.

In other words, nobody likes to be told what to do. Everyone wants to feel like something was their own idea rather than feeling like someone sold them. Mentioning why the neighbors bought creates more of a *buying environment* rather than a *selling environment.*

You can say things like, "What Cobi loved the most…" and "The reason Cobi switched to us is because…" Notice how you are not directly telling them what to do. Instead, you're 'shouldering off' with them and explaining why others have chosen to use you.

This keeps the conversation theoretical. It helps the homeowner feel more relaxed and contemplative, and now, they will be more willing to imagine themselves having your product/service.

But if you start telling them why *they* should buy, it can have an opposite effect. You usually haven't built up enough interest to apply that type of pressure.

'Bandwagoning' off of the nearby neighbors will utilize social conformity. This is a great way to hook interest and then continue to build it. It's far more powerful to make this a neighborhood thing rather than just focusing on the single homeowner you're talking to. This applies throughout the entire conversation, not just during your introduction.

My grandpa had a door-to-door pest control guy knock on his door once. The rep had inspected the house prior to knocking. When my grandpa came outside to talk, the rep pointed out a mud dauber nest and some other pest 'problems' that the house had. He tried showing all the reasons as to why my grandpa should buy.

What you need to understand is that homeowners usually already know what 'problems' they have. They don't need anyone pointing them out.

I'm not saying that you shouldn't pay close attention to specific details about each house; I'm just saying that there are better ways to utilize that information. You can mention these same challenges *that the neighbors* have been dealing with.

If you see a specific 'problem' when walking up to a house, then make a mental note of it as a 'hot button.' Mention that neighbors have been dealing with that specific hot button, so what they've loved the most is ... whatever your service is.

The goal is to utilize the neighbors in order to make the sale an open conversation rather than a closed confrontation.

If the homeowner has a really bad ant problem in his kitchen then tell him, "Cobi gets ants in his kitchen too. What he loves the most is that we do both outdoor *and* indoor treatments, and we'll always come back to perform free reservices if needed."

You're essentially making the argument that buying is the obvious decision. It's like peer pressure but without the negative connotation. You're indirectly telling homeowners that if their neighbors are doing it, then they should too, because their neighbors have already made the decision to trust you and make you a credible source.

This becomes very powerful as you mention the 'group rate.' This is how you create urgency in a lot of door-to-door selling.

You can say that the group rate is a limited-time offer 'while you're in the neighborhood' (which is the truth). If they have a high level of interest, then you'll have high odds of closing them.

Using social influences will help you build their interest while also building credibility around yourself. It will ease you into the sales dialogue and then allow you to be more direct later on.

With Great Power...

What I want to reiterate about the introductory part of the sale is the amount of influence that it contains. Although 'obedience to authority' can seem far-fetched, a lot of people will submit to your request as long as you nail your introduction.

There will be a lot of people who need or want what you're selling, so at this point, they just want to know what the price is before giving you their credit card.

This is because you've successfully convinced them that you're credible and uniquely different from other solicitors.

After mastering the art of manipulating snap judgments, you will then find yourself in more situations where *you* are the one who is quickly qualifying the other person. Most people will respect you enough to listen to what you have to say, so you don't want to waste your time talking with non-buyers.

Ask questions and test their level of engagement. Move on as soon as you know that they're not interested. Over time, you will acquire quick intuition that allows you to accurately filter out the non-buyers from the potential buyers. You will find yourself having more positive interactions and more productive conversations.

The ideal introduction should include: the reason you're there, the close neighbors who are currently customers, the discount that you're offering and an engaging question to test their level of interest.

CHAPTER 12:
SELLING YOUR PRODUCT/SERVICE

Both presidential candidates stood on their podiums, taking turns smearing each other and selling dreams to the American people. They often chuckled and shook their heads while the other candidate spoke.

In college, did you ever watch a presidential debate with friends over a few drinks? If you did, then I'm sure at least a couple of you became less shy about your political opinions. My friends certainly did.

Two of my friends happened to be very politically opinionated, but they supported opposite parties. You can already imagine where the conversation went. The interesting part was how each of them had retained different pieces of information provided during the debate.

Both of them had only retained the information that confirmed existing beliefs, while ignoring information that seemed to discredit their beliefs. Any argument that one candidate had obviously won was immediately forgotten and/or discredited by the friend who held the opposite political stance.

There was never a time where common ground was discovered, or even a time when one friend would seek to get a better understanding of the other person's point of view. There was just resistance and the strengthening of opposite opinions; there was no overlap or acknowledgment of an opposing argument that provided room for a productive discussion. They'd both just reinforced their existing beliefs, and gone on to describe the debate in two completely different ways.

This was a perfect example of 'confirmation bias.' This finding explains how we as humans notice things that confirm our existing beliefs, and ignore things that disconfirm our existing beliefs.

Confirmation bias is why it's important to stack multiple pieces of evidence that could subtly tackle the homeowner's event schema in the first few seconds.

This is also why it's important to maintain the positive snap judgment throughout the rest of the sale.

If you fall victim to a negative snap judgment, then the homeowner will begin to only notice things that confirm their stereotype. They will cherry pick information that reinforces their negative snap judgment of you.

Maintaining the Positive Snap Judgment

Be aware that a positive snap judgment can come tumbling down if you're not careful.

After your introduction, you must resist the urge to rush through your pitch.

Rushing through your pitch makes the conversation one-sided. It isn't at all considerate of the homeowner. They'll frequently tune out or cut you off if you dump information onto them before even trying to create a mutual conversation.

Think of it from the homeowner's perspective - it's kind of repulsive to come to their door and make them listen to a canned pitch without conversing with them first. This won't show much empathy or build rapport. They'll quickly lose interest if your pitch isn't chopped up with opportunities for them to talk as much - or as little - as they'd like.

In order to make it a mutual conversation, the script needs to include specific times for you to ask questions that are related to the overall sales dialogue. The good news is that you can ask the same exact one (or two, three, etc.) immediately after your introduction.

This has multiple benefits, some of which we've already talked about:

1) It engages them and doesn't seem like a stereotypical sales pitch.

2) It helps you qualify them.
3) It activates neurochemicals in their brain.
4) It helps you gain useful information.
5) It makes them more willing to reciprocate in conversation.

This last part is called the 'law of reciprocity.' When others do a good deed for us, we have a natural tendency to want to return the favor.

Asking questions and listening is often reciprocated in conversation. It also helps you to stay in control as you generate a conversation. This will usually make the homeowner more likely to disclose their buying likelihood, and more willing to transition further into sales dialogue.

Creating engagement will also help you maintain the perception that you're not like past solicitors; you're unique and personable.

It gives you time to mirror the homeowner and get closer to their 'in' group.

This will speed up the rapport-building process and make them more willing to share their unique situation.

Getting the homeowner to disclose useful information will help you decide which parts of your pitch are even worth talking about. It earns you the right to offer a catered message. You'll know how to specifically raise their level of interest by targeting what they're most likely to care about.

Also, if you rush through your pitch and rehearse *everything* that you've memorized, then you'll run out of influential information. Other than making it obvious to the homeowner that you're rehearsing a script, you'll run out of 'ammo' that you could have used later on.

This is a difficult lesson for new reps to learn since they typically have a harder time attaining a positive snap judgment. So, when they eventually find a homeowner who's interested enough to listen, they either forget what to say or they get eager and rush through the pitch.

Reps often haven't practiced prioritizing the interaction.

They haven't gotten comfortable with chopping up the pitch, asking useful questions and cherry picking relevant information.

If they've only rote-rehearsed it in practice, then it's easy for them to forget where to pick up at - and what to say - when the conversation gets jumbled.

New reps need to practice asking more questions and allowing for natural sales dialogue to sprout. Then they can pick and choose relevant information from the script. This catering process will continue to build the rapport that naturally comes about from prioritizing the conversation and the overall interaction.

Savvy door-to-door sales reps don't need to rely on the pitch to make them sales. Instead, they rely on

the experience that they provide while using the script as a tool.

If you master the art of your first impression, you'll come across some homeowners who don't even need to hear many details of your pitch. If they're highly interested in what you're selling, they'll trust you enough to buy after hearing the price and asking a question or two.

Obviously, this doesn't mean that you won't have to use the script to get sales (you almost always have to use it). This just means that you need to think of the script as a tool, and nothing more.

The script doesn't sell people. You sell people. Simply rote-rehearsing a script is not realistic when dealing with another human.

When you practice the pitch with another person, try making it a back and forth conversation after your introduction. Make sure you ask questions during the role-play, and generate natural dialogue. Gain information and then use that to cater your pitch accordingly.

A lot of new reps will not practice like this, and are very underprepared for their first official day. They're used to role-plays that don't entail realistic responses from the person acting as the homeowner (other than 'soft ball' objections).

So, on their first day knocking live doors, they're hit with the brutal realization of how hard it is to sell something to a stranger on their doorstep. They realize that maintaining control of the conversation is a lot harder when the other person is trying to end it as quickly as possible. Oftentimes, they won't know how to respond because they haven't proactively prepared for this reality.

The one asking the questions is the one in control.

This is why it's important to ask a question at the end of your introduction, and then memorize responses to different smokescreens. This keeps you in control, and directs the homeowner to engage on the topic that you're pushing for.

Remember that every detail of your brief interaction with homeowners will be magnified in their heads. Regardless of how good your product/service is, they'll never want to buy from somebody they don't like or trust.

If you talk too much, don't ask questions and don't listen well, then this will likely lead to negative attributions about you as a person. If you fidget or move around too much, then they'll perceive you as nervous and/or lacking confidence. If your introduction isn't right to the point, they'll probably think you're a stereotypical solicitor.

However, if you're confident and empathetic in your approach, then you'll raise your odds of gaining closer access to the homeowner's 'in' group. They'll feel disarmed by your demeanor and be less hesitant to engage in authentic sales dialogue. They'll even be more curious about what you have to offer.

You've probably heard this before and it's absolutely true - people buy with emotion and then justify with logic.

By asking questions, listening and generating a conversation, you'll release oxytocin and dopamine in their brain. This creates a more emotionally positive experience, and gives you a fighting chance to increase the quality and the scarcity of your offer.

This is exactly why you want to generate positive emotions - in yourself and the homeowner - before you start pitching on logic.

CHAPTER 13:
QUESTIONS REQUIRED, NO EXCEPTIONS

Remember how easy it was to tune out in class when your teacher or professor was lecturing? Now, compare that to a time when they called on students at random to answer questions. Your level of attention likely intensified.

This is exactly why you want to engage the homeowner with questions. It gets their brain firing and it gets them to talk and disclose information.

The average human attention span is about eight seconds long, and even now, it's declining (for context, it was around twelve seconds in the year 2000).

It's extremely important to involve the homeowner in the conversation sooner rather than later. If they tune out, then they'll lose interest, and their psychology will start working against you rather than for you.

The act of talking (and anticipation of talking) activates a dopamine reward in our brain when we successfully portray how we're thinking and/or feeling. This is what you must quickly activate within the homeowner in order to keep their attention and slide into sales dialogue.

Asking questions is also one of the most powerful rapport building tools. It can portray 'radical curiosity,' and show that you care to learn about the other person.

At the psychiatric hospital, portraying radical curiosity towards each individual patient was the best way to become an influential figure in their life. Showing that you cared enough to listen and to see things from their perspective was more powerful than anything you could say.

Although this is a lot deeper than door-to-door sales interactions, the same principle applies to homeowners wanting to feel like you care about getting to know their unique situation. It will help your commission breath not stink so bad.

I encourage you to try this with somebody in your life. Ask them about something that you know they care about and *listen*. Then dig deeper and ask them another question about something they said. Give them all of your attention without interrupting them or one-upping them.

The best type of question to ask is an open-ended question.

An open-ended question usually starts with either 'how' or 'what' because it doesn't leave as much room for a one-word response. In other words, it requires the person to elaborate.

For example, when I first started selling door-to-door pest control, I would often ask homeowners the question "*who* do you use for the bugs?" and they would almost always respond with either the name of a company, "my husband," or "me." This left little room for elaboration and imagination on the homeowner's part.

It wasn't until I became more familiar with open-ended questions that I changed my question to, "*what* do you do about the bugs?" Now, instead of imagining *who* got rid of the bugs, they had to imagine the bugs and the *act* of getting rid of them.

Quick side note - If you're selling pest control, then using 'who' isn't bad. It's fine if you're in a highly competitive area where most homes have a service already. The assumptive nature of the question can be powerful. It's something to play around with, but in my specific market, I found that 'what' was a better option.

The homeowner's response was usually a good indication of where they fell on the spectrum between 'non-buyer' and 'potential buyer.' Also, the information they disclosed was helpful in deciding what direction to take the conversation (Did they have a service already? Would they rather DIY? Did they have ants crawling up their kitchen walls?).

So now, after your introduction, you have options. You can ask, 'you're gonna be here tomorrow, right?' You can ask, 'who/what do you do about the bugs?' You can ask any question you prefer or questions that are fitting to your product/service.

Questioning is meant to catapult you further and further into a mutual conversation.

It helps you build rapport and then cater to their unique situation. Sometimes, you'll only have to ask one question, and sometimes, you'll have to ask more. I've found that it never hurts to ask another question before diving into relevant parts of the pitch.

In door-to-door sales, you want to figure out the homeowner's 'hot button(s).' These are also called 'pain points.' In pest control, for example, you want to figure out what pest annoys them the most; then you can cater your message around that specific pain point.

However, after learning about their hot buttons, you still want to ask more questions. You want to make the homeowner elaborate on their hot buttons in order to intensify their pain/discomfort.

Imagine if they had spiders for instance. If a homeowner tells you that they have a bad spider problem, then ask them to elaborate (Are they black or brown? What size are they? Where in the house do you usually see them? How do you get rid of them?). This gets the homeowner to visualize their problem and feel the discomfort as much as possible, while also getting them to talk and open up more.

The point is that you want to invest the homeowner into the conversation by getting them to think, feel and engage as much as possible. The best way to do this is by asking purposeful questions.

If They're Slipping Away

Questions also work great if a homeowner - who was originally interested - begins to disengage or become less interested. When this happens, ask a question that sort of 'takes a step back.' For example, "how long have you lived in the home?" or "are you originally from the area?"

It's usually not best to get off topic, but sometimes, you need to reel people back in if they originally seemed interested. The goal is to relieve some of the sales pressure and then eventually guide the conversation back towards productive dialogue. This 'step back' can also show empathy and give you a chance to build a sense of rapport.

After they respond to your step back question, it can sometimes be good to give a quick snippet about yourself. This can add quality to the conversation by making you seem more personable.

I used to mention my work at the psychiatric hospital. It gave me a sense of uniqueness, and I found that homeowners would usually engage on a more honest level afterwards. This helped me further qualify their buying likelihood as we got back into sales dialogue.

Remember that the one asking the questions is the one who's in control.

Questions give you the ability to maintain control, qualify people quickly, gauge their interest level, disclose hot buttons, raise their interest level, boost oxytocin and dopamine, build rapport, trigger the law of reciprocity, etc. The list goes on.

Returning Questions with Questions

It sounds like a power trip, but it's often good practice to respond to a homeowner's question by asking them a question in return.

For example, let's say that you finish your introduction and the homeowner asks you, 'what's half-off?' If you're selling pest control, then a good question to ask in return would be, 'what's the square footage of your house?'

This question will vary depending on what you're selling, but the point is that you want to be the one asking the questions. If the homeowner asks you, 'What do you do about mice?' then you can ask, 'Where are you seeing the mice?'

It never hurts to ask more questions, and it's always a good idea to stay in control of the conversation. If you start answering questions without asking one in return, then it can be easy to lose your sense of authority. This isn't a rule that you have to die by, but it's good to remember because it's more influential than you might think.

CHAPTER 14:
LISTEN, LEARN, LEVERAGE

D o you feel listened to? Do you feel like certain people in your life take the time to fully understand you? When you talk, do they seem genuinely curious in what you're saying? Or do they just seem to be focusing on what they're going to say next?

When you tell certain people about a current success of yours, do they celebrate this success with you without taking your spotlight away? When you speak of a failure or a current struggle, do they listen without cutting in or trying to correct you?

There aren't very many good listeners in the world. Better yet, there are too many people in the world who feel as though they aren't listened to. Too many people feel like they're not deeply understood because so few people truly take the time to be radically curious about them.

The amount of people seeking mental health treatment is going up, especially now during the pandemic. People spend thousands of dollars on counseling every single year.

Obviously, there are a lot of people who genuinely need to see a licensed counselor. I'm not saying that a door-to-door sales interaction is anything like a counseling session.

But the point I'm trying to make is this - how often do we truly absorb what somebody says to us without the intention of replying right away? How often do we give somebody our undivided attention without letting our ego jump into the conversation? How often do we dig deeper into what somebody tells us by asking another question?

My goal isn't to make people out to be selfish or horrible listeners - far from it, as most people listen empathetically on a daily basis. But the point is that people love to feel listened to and cared about. There is undeniably a lack of listening in way too many areas where there *should* be more listening: relationships, politics, sales, etc.

The more you listen to them, the more they will listen to you.

Obviously, there are important times to be the one talking, to challenge the homeowner, and to overcome objections, but this becomes a lot easier if you've taken the time to ask questions, listen and learn about their unique situation. This earns you the right to nudge them in the desired direction with an informed response.

Whenever I would role-play as the homeowner with new reps, I would mention that I only had ants. However, the new reps would still put just as much emphasis on spiders and wasps as they would on ants (since it was part of the script). They usually just breezed over ants as rehearsed, and they rarely ever asked me questions about them.

Putting emphasis on things that the homeowner doesn't care about - while ignoring things that they do - is less influential. It minimizes their hot button rather than amplifying it, and it makes them feel unheard. Talking about irrelevant perks and details wastes valuable time that should be spent on what the homeowner actually cares about.

If the homeowner discloses a hot button, then you need to milk it as much as you can.

Ask questions about it in order to show that you care to understand their unique issue. Then cater your pitch around it so that you don't just offer what seems to be a one-size-fits-all solution.

This is how you really get them engaged. This is how you build their interest and make them feel like you can meet their unique needs better than anyone else (without sounding like you're rehearsing a script).

It's okay to talk about other details of your product/ service, but wait until later on in the sale. Wait until you feel as though you need to raise their interest level higher or you've discovered another potential hot button. You should never have to rote-rehearse the script unless the homeowner is unwilling to share information (while obviously interested).

One of my favorite door-to-door memories was with a 65-year-old lady who lived alone. She was taking advantage of her opportunity to talk to somebody who listened, and was obviously enjoying her time doing so.

She kept going on and on about things that started to get off topic. She talked about COVID, the government, her spirituality, worldly evils, etc. My attempts at bringing the conversation back to sales dialogue kept failing, as she would quickly get right back to whatever topic she found more interesting.

I let her go on for a few minutes before deciding that I needed to push the conversation along (or at least not let it take up anymore of my time). I'd barely been able to get through my introduction, and she shrugged off the idea of a discount.

In order to dismiss myself from the conversation, I did the one thing that I was sure would get her to want me off of her porch - I closed her. "So should I start in the front yard, or would you rather I start the service in the backyard?"

She looked at me for a second, obviously taken aback, until she cracked a smile and replied with, "The front yard works fine." Then she continued talking like she'd never stopped. It took a long time to get the contract filled out, but in the end, it was worth it.

Every interaction is a little bit unique. It's very likely that this woman would have never bought from me if I hadn't taken the time to listen to her. Sometimes, taking the time to listen to somebody - unless you know for a fact that they won't buy - can have a very powerful effect.

As a reiteration, remember to resist the urge to rush through your pitch.

Avoid rambling and talking over the other person. This signifies insecurity and a lack of self-control. If you can't control yourself, how are you supposed to control the conversation and the sale?

The one who talks the most is not always the one who is in control of the conversation; it is the one asking the questions, listening, and speaking when necessary.

When you do speak, speak with confidence and authority. When the other person is disagreeing or saying 'no,' then smile, nod, listen and act like you were expecting them to say this.

Maintain a calm demeanor and body language to communicate your understanding and your position. Avoid cutting in and 'word vomiting' because this will make you seem insecure or like you're in panic mode. This will repel the homeowner and solidify their decision. Don't let their objections or concerns affect you visually or mentally.

Instead, just calmly wait for them to finish. Consider asking them a question to get a better understanding of their position, and then confidently respond while continuing to assume the sale. The other person will be much more likely to listen when you portray confidence rather than insecurity.

CHAPTER 15:
KNOWING WHEN, AND HOW, TO TALK ABOUT PRICE

Seclusion rooms weren't padded. The floors, ceilings and walls were all made of concrete. Behind the years of stains and markings, they were usually painted either a dark blue or a dark green.

On the outside, the seclusion door had five sliding locks. At head height, there was a 12-inch by 12-inch shatterproof window with small auditory holes for communication when the patient would be calm and compliant.

Patients weren't put in straitjackets. However, they weren't let out of seclusion until they had shown safe behavior and a willingness to follow directions. It was part of the debriefing protocol, after a patient required restraint and seclusion due to unsafe behavior.

In an ideal situation, we would restrain a patient until they calmed down and agreed to calmly walk into the seclusion room. This could take anywhere from two seconds to two hours.

The seclusion room was a needed area for escalated patients. If you will, it was how they would 'pay the price' after being restrained for unsafe behavior. I put quotes around 'pay the price,' because I want you to take this with a grain of salt.

Seclusion was never used as a punishment. It was used as a safety precaution for patients to calm down and display safer behavior. It was part of the process of trusting them to be safe around others again.

The *more* escalated the patient was while being restrained, the less they would be willing to 'pay the price' of seclusion. However, the *less* escalated the patient became, the more willing they would be to 'pay the price.' Their willingness to walk into seclusion was directly correlated with the intensity of their emotional state.

Although you're not going to physically restrain homeowners until they give you their credit cards, at some point, you're going to have to talk about price in order to make the sale. And like the psychiatric hospital, homeowners are going to be less willing to talk about price if they still have a low level of interest.

Knowing *when* to talk about price depends on the homeowner's interest level. I was taught to talk about price early (after the intro) and sort of 'get it out of the way,' but this strategy doesn't work best for every situation. This typically works better for homeowners who are immediately interested after your introduction.

The more interested they are, the more willing they'll be to justify the price. The less interested they are, the less willing they'll be to justify the price.

At the end of your introduction, if the homeowner is excited, engaging, and/or asking questions, then this is usually a good sign that they're interested. These are called 'buying signs,' which can easily guide you into a price discussion.

Sometimes, if the homeowner judges you positively and has a want/need for what you're selling, they'll be sold as soon as you tell them the price. They'll quickly show obvious buying signs that allow you to slide right into filling out the contract with them.

However, there will also be times when you need to mention most details of your product/service before the homeowner will seem interested enough to talk about price. It all depends on the specific person.

Just don't get caught up in the idea that every homeowner needs to know every detail of the pitch.

New reps often lose easy sales because they talk too much. The homeowner will be sold at point A, but the rep continues to go through point B, C and D because they're conditioned to do so.

If the homeowner is sold after your introduction and price, then close them and fill out the contract. Continuing to pitch will leave room for potential error.

A door-to-door sale is typically an *impulse buy*, so don't allow any extra time for them to possibly change their mind.

On the flip side, talking about price *without* the interest of the homeowner typically sets you up for failure. Why would somebody consider rationalizing the price of something when they're not interested enough yet?

Most homeowners will fall into this ladder category. For them, you need to strategically ask questions and build a mutually beneficial conversation.

As you discover hot buttons, discover potential hesitations, build a sense of rapport, and cater a unique pitch, you'll have a higher likelihood of the homeowner justifying the price (or at least sticking around to negotiate it).

The critical process for raising a homeowner's interest involves questioning, information gathering, digging into hot buttons and cherry-picking from the script.

Anchoring and Adjustment

A powerful psychological trick used when describing price is called 'anchoring and adjustment.' This is simple, and it plays a role in our lives almost every day.

If you're at a store and see an item that's 'on sale,' the store will make sure that you see both the original price (the anchor) and the new discounted price (the adjustment). The original price is meant to set a mental anchor in your head, and will then make the discounted price seem more attractive. An anchor raises the product's value while also giving more power to the adjusted price.

Anchoring and adjustment is very common in price negotiations. For example, if you need to quickly sell your car for $20,000 then you wouldn't have this be your first offer. Instead you would offer something higher.

You might say that your car is worth $30,000, but if they buy it right now, then you'll sell it for just $25,000. This leaves you room to negotiate the price lower if needed, and builds value in a final offer of only $20,000.

You cannot lose from starting high and bargaining lower.

It builds value and leaves you room to negotiate. It also engages the other person and gives them a sense of agency in the buying process.

Anchoring and adjustment is probably already implemented into the introduction of your script. If it isn't, then you need to add it. This is where you initially hook the homeowner's interest.

It's important to reiterate, though, that they won't be receptive to your discount if they didn't have a positive snap judgment of you in the first place. They'll be more likely to perceive the discount as a scam, or think that you have stereotypical commission breath.

But assuming that you did influence their snap judgment to your favor, you will usually end your intro with something along the lines of 'half off' or 'group rate.' If you're selling a service, then I highly recommend using 'group rate' and attributing it to a neighborhood discount.

You can say something like, "Since I'm already gonna be here for the neighbors I take care of, if you can be here as well, then I'll get you in to the group rate that they have together. It's half of the normal price. You're gonna be here in a couple hours, right?"

Remember your paraverbal communication because this is a *very* important ending to your intro.

Make sure to slow down at "group rate," and begin slightly lowering your voice when you get to "it's half," so that you sound absolutely certain about the scarcity of the information. You can then use a casual tone of voice again when you ask if they'll be there in a couple hours.

The changes in your voice don't need to be overly dramatic. They just need to be subtle enough for the homeowner to pick up on them. Remember that *how* you say this is just as important as *what* you're actually saying.

Also, notice the question at the end. It's assumptive, and it forces the homeowner to engage. How they respond will typically disclose their level of interest.

Will they ask what the group rate is? Will they tell you that 'yes,' they will be home? Will they tell you that 'no,' they won't be home? Will they disregard the question and tell you that they're not interested?

Depending on their response, you can go right into price, you can ask them another question, or you can move on to the next house if they're definitely a non-buyer.

Remember that this is a common time to be told some sort of smokescreen. For whatever reason, the homeowner is usually uncertain and not yet willing to consider your offer. This is when you want to put emphasis on how the discount is 'now or never.'

Unless they're not the decision maker of the home – and they need you to come back at a specific time to talk to whoever is – then you need to make it apparent that this is not a 'call-in' discount.

Never leave a card or your cell phone number.

I made this mistake many times during my first summer and nobody ever called me back after 'thinking' about it. Wanting to 'think about it' is a smokescreen for uncertainty. Homeowners will never think themselves into it without your influence.

Rather than walk away and cross your fingers, you need to raise their level of certainty. Door-to-door sales are impulsive purchases that homeowners will almost always think themselves out of.

Don't leave any stone unturned, and don't fall victim to any smokescreens unless you're absolutely certain that it's the only option.

Loss Aversion

Another reason to be willing to walk away with your discount has to do with a psychological finding called 'loss aversion.' Loss aversion explains part of how humans perceive pain versus pleasure.

For example, the pain of potentially losing $100 is typically stronger than the pleasure of potentially gaining $100. When a homeowner is genuinely interested but lacking enough certainty to pull the trigger, it's best to frame your offer in terms of a potential loss.

'Missing out' on a limited time discount will have more influence than 'taking advantage of' a limited time discount.

People are typically more motivated to work in order to avoid pain than they are to work in order to attain pleasure. You can utilize this understanding to motivate others into action. Combining loss aversion with social conformity is directly related to the 'Keeping up with Joneses' concept.

For example, let's say that a homeowner asks you to 'leave a card' after your introduction. A good response would be something like, "I would, but unfortunately, it's not a call-in discount. I don't want anyone to miss out on the group rate and then possibly have to pay the full price later on. What do you typically do about the bugs?"

Price Dropping

Price dropping can be one of your most powerful tools if it's done correctly. Door-to-door usually involves a lot of bargaining and price dropping, so it's important to start high and then slowly dwindle lower.

Don't be too quick to drop to your lowest price.

Other than the initial discount in your introduction, you should typically avoid offering other large price drops. Doing so has multiple downsides.

Other than having much less room to negotiate, continuing to offer huge discounts will decrease the perceived value of your product/service. Painlessly dropping too low, too quickly, is typically a red flag for desperation and low quality. It can make your commission breath stink even worse.

If the initial 'half-off' discount in your introduction doesn't 'wow' the homeowner, then continuing to offer bigger discounts isn't your best route. Your best route towards gaining their interest will be through conversation, catering parts of your pitch and incrementally negotiating the price later on.

It's okay to dwindle your price down low, but it needs to be done gradually rather than drastically. The best way to drop the price is by giving another small discount after each time you're told 'no.'

A great way to deliver a price drop is by acting as though it 'hurts' to do so. You can give this impression by sighing or looking down at your iPad for a few seconds; what's important here is that you make it seem as though you're going out on a limb for the customer.

Pro tip – When you drop the price, explain the new discount in a way that *makes sense* (especially if it's a bigger price drop).

You need to justify your willingness to give another discount. This is when you, again, can use the neighbors as a reference.

For example, in pest control, a lot of homeowners already use a different service. In order to get them to switch over to yours, you usually have to pro-rate the first service that you do for them. This big price drop on their first service is needed since they recently paid their other company for a service.

So when I did need to 'wow' a homeowner who *did not* already have a service, I would say something like, "Tell you what. Your neighbor Cobi just switched to me from Psychiatric Pest Control, so I had to pro-rate his first service all the way down to just 55 bucks. If you fill one of these last couple spots, then I'll start you off at 55 bucks as well. Sound fair enough?"

Although it was a big price drop, there was authentic reasoning to doing so. Just remember to use big price drops like this only under the right circumstances, because the lower you go, the less room you have to negotiate.

CHAPTER 16

THE ART AND SCIENCE OF CLOSING THE DEAL

still had zero sales on a rainy afternoon in Portland, OR. After a quick lunch, I finally found a homeowner who I engaged in a productive conversation. He showed curiosity as he answered my questions and disclosed that he had an ant problem.

Ultimately, though, he was unwilling to pull the trigger no matter what I did. I tried giving multiple discounts and closing multiple times but nothing worked. I got to the point where I couldn't waste any more time, so I moved on to his neighbor's house.

His neighbor ended up being a very easy sale. On top of that, I found out that both of them had a rat problem (something that the first guy never told me about). I immediately went back to the first guy's house and knocked his door again. He was slow to answer, and when he finally did respond, he had an annoyed look on his face.

After name-dropping his neighbor, presenting the solution to the rat problem, and offering another discount, he bought. I took the momentum from those two sales and ended the day with nine in total.

Closing is the bread and butter of door-to-door sales.

You're probably familiar with the saying 'Always Be Closing' (ABC) because it's true in a lot of ways. You need to have the confidence to close and the experience to know how to do it properly.

Although it can seem awkward or forceful at first, you will learn that customers feel awkward when you *do not* close them. If you have maintained your positive snap judgment, gone over price, and raised their interest level, then closing should be the most natural part of the sale.

However, odds are that they will tell you 'no' after your first close.

This should never catch you by surprise.

Getting told 'no' is often a good thing because it paves the way for disclosure and negotiation. It allows you to overcome the true concern and leverage your rapport with the homeowner.

This is where you earn your money. This is where you master the art of pleasant persistence, negotiation and influence.

There are ways to close someone four, five, even six or more times without being aggressive or annoying. There are ways to maintain rapport and be pleasantly persistent without being a people-pleaser or a push-over.

You're not in door-to-door sales to make friends. You're in door-to-door sales to influence people to the point of buying. If you truly believe that your product/service is great, then you will have no problem pushing through 'nos' multiple times in a single conversation.

It's important that you understand how to be pleasantly persistent during the back half of the sale. My goal is to highlight the best types of closes for common situations, and to show you how to utilize specific psychological factors.

This section will disclose how to implement specific closing strategies in a way that engages the homeowner and gradually leverages the law of reciprocity.

I don't intend to overwhelm you with various types of closes. Instead, I plan to teach you a framework that is highly effective with homeowners. For starters, it's important to explain the difference between 'soft closes' and 'hard closes.'

Soft Close

"You're gonna be here in a couple hours, right?" Along with being an assumptive question, this is also an example of a soft close. It's a micro-commitment that primes interested homeowners with the assumptive belief that being home is in their best interest.

In general, a soft close is a 'warm up.' It subtly nudges the homeowner in the desired direction.

This works best for homeowners who have not yet disclosed their level of interest. That's why it's placed at the end of the introduction. It tests their level of interest without being too aggressive.

A close is always assumptive in nature, but a soft close is just subtler about it.

You want to see how much the homeowner will 'play along' with the conversation. Their response will usually disclose where they fall on the spectrum between 'very interested' and 'not at all interested.'

Soft closes work great with people who are on the fence or who have a lower level of certainty. They need to be nudged without feeling like they're being pressured. This makes them become more decisive or at least transparent about their thoughts.

When I was selling pest control, my most affective soft close was, "other than the ants, what else could we take care of for you?" I would then hold out a picture of our pest chart for them to look at.

This would visually engage them and usually make them disclose more hot buttons. It would generate more sales dialogue and help me to raise their interest level.

The worst thing that can happen is that they shut the conversation down. They back off and tell you the truth behind their reason for saying 'no.'

This isn't a bad thing, though. Getting to the truth saves you time and helps you decide what your next move should be. Should you move on to the next house or should you work to overcome their objection?

The goal is to gauge their interest level and discover their true hesitations.

Remember that soft closing is best for the homeowners that have an unclear interest level. If you were to try and hard close somebody at this level, they would likely back off, feel pressured, and be less honest about their reason for saying 'no.'

Hard Close

Hard closing is primarily what reps are taught because it's the best way to close highly interested homeowners. Hard closes are straightforward, and ideally how you want to solidify your sales.

The most basic type of hard close is called a 'contract close.' With a contract close, you ask for a piece of information about the homeowner that you then use to start filling out the contract.

For example, "I just need some basic information to get you started, what's your last name?" or "what's a good email that I can send the agreement over to?"

An 'option close' and an 'assignment close' are two other examples of hard closes. An option close is when you give somebody the choice to pick between two options, both of which assume that they're going to buy. For example, "should I start the service in the front yard or the back-yard?" or "Does 1pm or 3pm work better for you?"

An assignment close is when you assign a task to the customer, which entails them buying the service. For example, "Will you open the garage when we get here? The garage treatment is included" or "Will you leave your dog inside while we're working? He can come right back outside when we're done."

Hard closes are best when the homeowner shows high levels of interest and certainty.

Different types of hard closes are important to remember so that you don't give the same type to the same person more than once. Mixing up the type of close that you use will prevent you from sounding repetitive, and will in turn prevent the homeowner from feeling pressured.

I would typically start with a soft close after the introduction, possibly use another soft close during the conversation, and then use a hard close after going over the service and the price.

In door-to-door sales, you're rarely able to ask for permission and expect the homeowner to agree. More often than not, their way of saying 'yes' is when they follow along with one of your closes.

You need to reach out and take sales, not ask permission for them.

If you ask permission, then homeowners will think of any reason to back out. Asking permission shows a lack of confidence on your part, and will make homeowners second-guess their own certainty.

Remember that an authority figure doesn't ask for permission. They assume that others will obey without hesitation. You don't want to give the homeowner an opportunity to hesitate.

As a recap – at this point, you've maintained a positive snap judgment, you've built a conversation, you've catered a relevant pitch, you've gone over price, and you've been told 'no' after your first close. How do you continue on from here?

This is the most crucial part of a sale. This is what will separate the average-performing reps from the high-performing reps.

Are you able to push through 'no' a couple of times while maintaining the rapport that you've built? Are you able to keep the negotiation pleasant while still being influential and nudging the homeowner in the right direction?

I promise that it's not as hard as it sounds. If the homeowner is still standing there and willing to talk to you, then you still have a high likelihood of closing them.

Other than work ethic, this is the skill that sets apart the great reps from the good reps. Are you able to maintain enough rapport with a stranger to blatantly push through 'nos' without losing your positive snap judgment?

There are tricks to help you get to this point, which is exactly what you're going to learn next.

CHAPTER 17:
HOW TO DOUBLE YOUR CLOSING RATE

Seriously, do you want to double your closing rate? Do you want to figure out how to be pleasantly persistent rather than pushy in the back half of a sale?

This can be accomplished. The method of doing so isn't traditionally taught in door-to-door settings, though, because you typically *need* to be pushy.

So how do you push without applying too much pressure? How do you close multiple times without the homeowner becoming annoyed or turned off? And how do you do so in a way that uses psychology to your advantage?

It's hard to push through multiple 'nos' without seeming aggressive or desperate, and homeowners will usually say 'no' at least once before they say 'yes.' This is why it's very important to implement a closing strategy that includes pleasant persistence and the law of reciprocity.

The goal is to make the homeowner feel like you're 'going out on a limb' to help them. They need to have a positive perception of your persistence, instead of thinking that you're only trying to make a commission.

So, how do you do this?

The quick answer is, you don't want to continue using hard closes. Continuing to use heavily assumptive closes will usually become less and less 'pleasant' each time you try.

I'm going to assume that you've heard of the Resolve, Ace and Close (RAC) method. This is the general formula for resolving real concerns and closing homeowners in the back half of the sale.

However, there is a specific way that this method should be applied when pushing through 'no' more than once. We'll go over 'resolve' in the next chapter. For now, let's focus on 'ace' and 'close.'

How do you ace and close somebody multiple times without coming off as aggressive or overly pushy? It's actually simple. It involves incremental price drops and *the same close every single time.*

I understand that this is contradictory to what I mentioned about closing earlier, so let me explain. Let's assume that you used a soft close and a hard close, and then you were told 'no.'

From here on out, you want to focus less on using assumptive closes. Instead, you want to transition into leveraging the law of reciprocity.

The good news is that you don't need to have multiple different hard closes memorized for when you try to close a homeowner a second, third or fourth time. Hard closes usually become counter-productive once you encounter resistance at this point in the sale.

This is the point in the sale when you want to close with "does that sound fair?" or "sound fair enough?"

These are the other words that you can almost call 'magic words' in door-to-door sales.

In addition to what I said before about the law of reciprocity, studies have found that the size of the favor asked in return doesn't matter. Humans will still have a hard time saying 'no,' even if the favor asked in return is costlier than the original good deed that was done for them.

For example, let's say that you buy someone lunch. Then after lunch you ask them if they can come over the next day to help you move out of your apartment. Their logical answer should be 'no,' since helping you move is much costlier than whatever you spent on their lunch.

However, studies show that the other person will still have a hard time saying 'no' to your asking. So, how does this relate to door-to-door sales and closing?

Let's run through an example. In this example, let's assume that you finished your pitch, used a hard close, the homeowner said 'no,' and you resolved whatever concern they had. You might try to close again by saying something like this.

"Tell you what. My trucks are going to be here for the next couple of hours anyway. If you fill one of these last spots, I'll take 40 more dollars off of your first service. Does that sound fair?"

"Hmm, yeah that sounds fair, but I still want to think about it. Can you leave me your card and I'll call you in an hour?"

"For sure. I understand that you want to make the best decision for your home. Is it the price or the commitment that you want to think more about?"

"It's the commitment. I don't want to be locked into a contract for two years."

"I hear you. I don't want you to feel locked into anything so I'll tell you what. If you give me a shot to earn your business then I'll put you on a one-year trial period. I usually reserve this for renters but I'll go ahead and do it for you anyway. Sound fair enough?"

"I don't know. I guess I'm still hung up on the price. I don't want to spend hundreds of dollars on pest control when I only get ants and spiders."

"Gotcha. How well do you know Cobi down the street?"

"Kind of, I see him walking his dog occasionally. Why?"

"Cobi has been using me for a few years now. His quarterly rates were lowered to just $119 because of his loyalty. If you promise not to tell some of the other neighbors, I'll go ahead and start you off at $119 instead of the $139. Does that sound fair?"

"Yeah that sounds fair."

"Awesome, what's a good email that I can send the service agreement over to?"

Notice how "sound fair enough?" and "does that sound fair?" doesn't become repetitive or pushy, and it doesn't breathe commission breath all over the homeowner. Instead, it signals that you're trying to create a solution that's fair by going out on a limb in the process of doing so.

Being overly assumptive isn't the goal anymore because it doesn't authentically engage the homeowner into a 'fair' negotiation. They will feel less and less obliged to consider your offers and engage in the conversation.

You maintain pleasant persistence by negotiating for a 'fair' agreement. This will build perceived value in the offer while simultaneously triggering the law of reciprocity within the homeowner.

Despite that you're only giving minor price drops (or agreement adjustments, add-ons, etc.) it can be very powerful when done correctly. Homeowners usually won't notice that what you're asking for (the sale) is a lot costlier than the incremental deeds you're giving (the price drops).

If you've gotten to this point with the homeowner, then odds are that they're still interested and able to be closed. They just need some more nudging and motivation to do so. This is how you do just that.

If they still hold a positive judgment of you, then their confirmation bias will be kicking in. They will perceive your negotiation as an attempt to help them rather than just make a commission.

Also, notice how I said "if you" in each one of my closes. This holds a lot of power in itself because it sets up your price drop more effectively. 'If you do this, then I will do this.'

'If you' subconsciously primes the homeowner to think that there is a trade-off rather than you just giving something for free.

Again, you don't want to seem desperate. You want to seem like you're trying to meet the homeowner where they're at and create a fair agreement.

Remember that you can sigh, look down at your iPad for a couple seconds, etc., before each price drop. This helps you 'sell' the fact that you're 'going out on a limb' for the homeowner. Acting plays a huge part in this point of the sale.

Keep a calm and confident posture when rolling through this process, and remember to smile and nod your head. Don't let the third, fourth or fifth 'no' negatively affect you. The fact that they're still willing to consider your offer is a great sign.

Also, remember your tonality when you're closing. Typically, you want to end on a low tone so that you sound confident and authoritative, but there is an exception with the close, "sound fair enough?"

This question naturally ends on an up tone, and is the only close that should end that way. Practice a few key closes until you've perfected your tonality for each one. This includes soft closes, hard closes and 'fair' closes.

The final close that I'd like to mention is called a 'confidence close.' The reason that I'm mentioning it last is because you shouldn't use it unless it's your last attempt at closing the homeowner.

You've already dwindled your price down low, yet, the homeowner is still on the fence and unwilling to pull the trigger. Here is an example of how you could offer a final 'confidence' close.

"Tell you what. I'll put my money where my mouth is. I'll literally do the first service for free, and drop your quarterlies down to just 109 bucks. I rarely ever go this low, but I really need to get this last spot filled on my route. All I ask is that you be here to see the work that I do. Sound fair enough?"

My rule is that you should always dwindle down to your lowest price before walking away from an interested homeowner, and that you should always tell them that it's your lowest price.

Promise yourself, right now, that you'll always give this final nudge before walking away. If you do, then you'll be surprised how many homeowners will end up buying.

Make sure to add some emotion to this last close. That's why it's called a 'confidence close.' You must be confident in your work (and your ability to sell) so that you can portray this to homeowners.

This is part of the acting. A genuine sense of confidence mixed with your best price can be hard for a lot of interested homeowners to turn down (especially when you've built a sense of rapport with them).

Remember to only use this type of close as a last resort, though. It can seem insincere or desperate if you do it too early. Using this towards the end is a way to cut through the bullshit and be as humanly honest as possible.

If the rapport is right, then using this will make it harder for the homeowner to tell you 'no.'

CHAPTER 18:
DOS AND DON'TS OF RESOLVING CONCERNS

"**I** want to think about it," "I need to talk to my husband/wife," "It's too expensive," "I don't like contracts," "I want to do more research," "I don't like chemicals," etc. Do these sound familiar?

Although concerns are typically more truthful than smokescreens, they're still partly excuses for uncertainty. You need to know how to respond to each one (as it relates to your product/service) during this back half of the sale.

Resolving concerns can be a fine line. Although you want to validate the concern, you don't want to give it too much weight. Although you want to challenge their thinking, you don't want to blatantly disagree with them.

Good team leaders and coaches will teach you how to rebuttal every common concern. However, you also need to know how to resolve common concerns *before* challenging them.

You need to memorize specific questions and validations that guide you into an effective resolve, ace and close (RAC).

Concerns like 'I want to think about it' and 'it's too expensive' usually need to be dug into and/or validated first. If you just seek to challenge and correct these types of concerns, the homeowner can feel pressured and/or misunderstood.

However, if the homeowner simply has a misunderstanding about your product/service, this can be easily corrected without needing to be carefully resolved.

For example, the concern 'I don't like chemicals' in pest control doesn't require questioning or validation if your company uses environmentally friendly products. This concern just requires you to educate the homeowner.

You can say, "That's what you'll love about my service. All of my products are certified as people, pet and plant-friendly. Will you just leave your dog inside while we're performing the service so that he doesn't lick us to death? He can come right back outside when we're done."

The goal is to have a prepared response for each concern. That way, you can smoothly transition into your ace and close.

Resolving with Questions and Validation

Validation is a counseling practice that's used to empower the client or patient. It's meant to be the first step in making somebody feel that you listen, understand and care. There are multiple levels of validation.

The first level is merely being present with the other person in conversation. Hopefully, you're present when talking with homeowners, meaning that you actively listen and absorb the things that they're telling you.

The second level is by reflecting back things that they say to you. For example, if somebody tells you "I want to think about it," then reflecting back "you want to make the best decision" would be an accurate reflection.

The third level of validation is when you actively reflect somebody's thought or emotional state based on the behavior that they're expressing. This is done without the other person verbally telling you. I'll touch more on this part later.

Accurate reflection and understanding can go a long way, as long as you quickly move on to your solution. You don't want to linger too long on a concern because it gives the concern too much weight. This might reinforce the concern.

But at the same time, you still want to acknowledge that you understand. Instead of disregarding the concern (like you would a smokescreen), you want to validate their thought/emotion, and then quickly resolve the concern with a solution.

This makes your solution more powerful because you're not disagreeing with the homeowner. You're simply offering them a new perspective.

For example, the 'I want to think about it' concern is arguably the most common concern given in sales. What this truly means is that they're not certain enough to say 'yes,' so you need to discover what they're most uncertain about and then begin to resolve it with a validation. Here's an example.

"I want to think about it."

"Of course, you want to make the best decision for your home. Is it the price or the commitment that you want to think more about?"

"It's the price. I don't think I can justify spending hundreds of dollars on pest control to my wife."

"Yeah, I don't want you sleeping on the couch tonight. What does your wife think about the bugs?"

"She hates the spiders. Screams every time she sees one."

"I bet. Most women want the bugs gone but they also want a good deal. I'll tell you what. Cobi just switched over to me from another company so I had to pro-rate his first service down to just 45 bucks. If you give me a shot to earn your business then I'll do the same for you. That way, you can justify it to your wife. Sound fair enough?"

This might require one or two more rounds of a resolve, ace and close, but you get the picture. Now, let's back up and assume that the only concern had been price.

"It's too expensive."

"I hear you, pest control can be expensive. That's why I don't want anyone to miss out on the group rate. So I'll tell you what. Some of the neighbors have been with me for a few years now and only pay 119 bucks per quarter. If you promise not to tell too many neighbors, I'll go ahead and start you off at that price. Does that sound fair?"

The point is that you want to be neutral and get to the truth. What's really holding the homeowner back? Is it the price, the commitment, the spouse or something/someone else? Once you figure that out, you want to validate the concern and then resolve it head on with an ace (usually a price drop).

Starting with validation makes the homeowner feel understood. It's a quick way to de-escalate their concern before confidently offering a solution.

It will make the homeowner more willing to consider your next offer, which then helps you leverage the law of reciprocity even further.

Remember that you need to attain and *maintain* your positive snap judgment. One of the quickest ways to lose this positive impression is by disregarding a homeowner's concerns and trying to pressure them into buying.

The way that you escape this perspective is by seeking to first understand and to validate. This will make you seem like you're working with them rather than pushing them to do something they don't want to do.

Resolving their underlying concern (and validating that concern) by going out on a limb to hook them up is exactly how you trigger the law of reciprocity.

This positive flow of energy is important in door-to-door sales, since the homeowner has the freedom to close the door at any time. You need to utilize this psychology with as many interested homeowners as possible.

Pigeonholing

There's another huge benefit to validating concerns and leveraging reciprocity. Before explaining what 'pigeonholing' is, let's go over the three possibilities at this point in the sale.

Possibility number one is that they buy. Possibility number two is that they don't buy. Possibility number three is that they lie.

In regards to possibility number three, their initial concern could have actually been a smokescreen in disguise. So, now that you've resolved their false concern, they're stuck in an awkward situation.

Let's assume that the homeowner goes with possibility number three. After you validate, resolve, ace and close this false concern, they'll then be more likely to go with either possibility number one or number two. They'll be much less likely to go with possibility three again (continuing to lie/smokescreen).

This is because you've successfully 'pigeonholed' the homeowner into a category that they don't want to be part of (inauthentic, untruthful, or etc.). They usually won't want to keep lying to you or keep giving you smokescreens.

Homeowners can often feel cognitive dissonance in these situations because they don't believe themselves to be untruthful or inauthentic (even though they were initially being that way towards you).

Usually, they'll change their behavior. They'll either buy your product/service or at least be more transparent with you about their real concern. Pigeonholing kind of sticks the homeowner 'between a rock and a hard place.'

Remember that people don't typically like conflict. Homeowners will have a hard time saying 'no' this late in the sale. It can be discomforting for them if they now have to admit that they were dishonest about their initial concern.

If the homeowner is genuinely interested, still holding a positive impression of you, and feeling obliged to reciprocate your good deeds, then you have a shot at them buying right then and there. Worst-case scenario is that they still say 'no,' but they tell you their *truthful reasoning.*

By validating, resolving, acing and closing, you're actively pigeonholing homeowners who were dishonest with you.

Most homeowners won't buy after being initially pigeonholed, and that's okay! It's part of the process of being pleasantly persistent. Once they tell you the true concern, you can then validate, resolve, ace and close that one too.

Some homeowners need this final nudge. They need you to push through their bullshit and create an authentic conversation.

Remember the sales funnel.

Although most homeowners won't buy, you can easily double your closing rate if you're able to be pleasantly persistent and leverage key psychological factors in the back half of the sale.

It takes practice, but it also starts with your own mentality.

Generating and maintaining positivity during a sale all depends on your own ability to stay calm, confident and optimistic. Don't let concerns affect your mentality or nonverbal communication in any negative way.

Also, remember that you can back up and make the conversation more personable if the homeowner is beginning to pull away. Sometimes, they'll begin to disengage or become less interested after you go through the closing process.

This relates to the third level of validation. It can be very helpful to read a homeowner's mental/emotional state and then reflect that in your response.

Ask them a semi-unrelated question or tell them a quick snippet about yourself. Get them re-engaged and then get back to the sales dialogue. Dwindle your price down until you've gotten to your lowest possible offer.

Remember that people buy based on the interaction. **They'll buy with emotion and then justify with logic, so sometimes you need to backup and generate more oxytocin and dopamine. Then you can get back to generating certainty with validation and reciprocation.**

Although this is heavy on *what* to say, I want to reiterate the fact that it goes a lot deeper than that. Other than non-verbals and paraverbals, it's about reading the other person and then *determining* what to say, and not just rehearsing a memorized pitch.

The more you sell door-to-door, the more you'll recognize situations and know exactly what to say ahead of time. **But there are multiple dimensions of situations that couldn't possibly be written into a single script.**

Your best bet is to learn the foundation of how to cater to another person. Make the interaction more about the homeowner rather than about the script.

Before you pitch, resolve, or close, make sure to get a better understanding of the homeowner's unique situation and interest level. Then reflect this understanding by catering your message.

CHAPTER 19:

HOW TO BE A TRUSTED ADVISOR

Have you ever been to therapy?

If you have, then you might know that there's a framework called 'motivational interviewing,' which is used to motivate and empower people to make a change. Again, you're not a counselor, but there are interesting similarities between counseling and selling.

In both, you're building rapport, empowering the other person, generating motivation and influencing behavior.

Motivational interviewing is best described by the acronym RULE:

1) Resist the urge to blatantly disagree.
2) Understand the other person's motivations.
3) Listen empathetically.
4) Empower the other person.

Let's start with the first part, 'Resist the urge to disagree.' There's a fine line between resolving and disagreeing.

When given a concern or told 'no,' start your response by nodding your head and saying "yeah," "of course," "I hear you," or something along those lines, so that there's less friction going into what you say next.

Staying in a constant state of agreement will subconsciously make the homeowner feel understood, and also make them more likely to agree with you as well - as long as you've maintained your positive snap judgment. This is a huge part of having pleasant persistence.

The second part of motivational interviewing is 'Understanding the other person's motivations.' This usually refers to the homeowner's hot buttons. You must cater to them in the same way that you cater to concerns.

The homeowner's main motivation could be their hot buttons, the discount, their desire to conform to the neighbors, or even the rapport that you've quickly established with them. You want to identify their motivation and utilize it as much as possible.

Next is 'Listen empathetically.' Remember that this is how you learn about hot buttons; make the homeowner trust you, build a reciprocating conversation, generate the proper neurochemicals, etc.

Lastly, we have 'Empower the other person.' Empowering the other person is done in many ways, most of which I've already gone over: limited time discount, catering the pitch, rapport, validation, resolving concerns, price dropping, solving hot buttons, the law of reciprocity, etc.

Empowerment is similar to encouragement. Every time you challenge the other person, you want to do it in a way that seems more like an encouragement than a disagreement. This is where pleasant persistence and the law of reciprocity come into play.

When you understand an individual's motivations, it becomes much easier to resolve their concerns and influence their behavior.

Remember how you want to maintain your positive snap judgment all the way through to the close. You accomplish this by listening, catering, validating, being pleasantly persistent and understanding their motivations. This will make your commission breath not stink so bad.

If you blatantly disagree with them, then you will create too much argumentative friction, and this will remind them of their initial event schema.

Resolving their concerns should be less about debate and more about empowerment and encouragement.

Although everybody is different in regards to their motivations, the truth is that everybody needs to be closed. You will occasionally run into 'lay down' sales, but they are rare. You cannot rely on them. You can only rely on yourself being as positive and as human as possible in your attempts to understand and influence others.

CHAPTER 20:

KNOCK, AND THE DOOR WILL BE OPENED TO YOU

It had been two weeks without a single sale. Everyone he started with had already made at least a few, but he was still at zero. He was given one more week to turn it around, or else he would be released from the team.

Believe it or not, that same rep went on to become one of the top sellers in the company. He went on to find massive success even though he found nothing but rejection during his first 100+ hours of door-to-door sales.

Getting comfortable with rejection and failure is an initiation process. Everybody goes through it. It's a way to weed out the quitters.

If you want to reap the rewards of door-to-door sales, then you're going to have to earn it. Nobody is naturally great when they first start. Gaining the necessary skills requires a rock-solid mentality and the perseverance to continuously learn.

A lot of people are unable to control their cognitive triangle throughout the process. They become negative and/or doubtful because it's hard to maintain abundant positivity and the initiative to always improve.

Homeowners will sense negativity and pessimism, and they will be repelled by it.

The only way to become great at door-to-door sales is by patiently expanding your sales funnel, little by little, every single day without becoming discouraged. This delayed gratification is a hard reality, and as a result, quitting often becomes more and more desirable.

Quitting is the biggest failure in door-to-door; coasting without improvement is a close second. A lot of reps get discouraged by continuous rejection because they haven't rationalized it as just being part of the process.

Even the best reps get rejected more often than not. Filtering out non-buyers is part of the game and should be implemented into your approach. That way, you can be prepared and positive when you're confronted with a potential buyer.

So how do you maintain positivity in your mindset and in your attitude? How do you continuously improve and persevere? It begins with the preparation that you make before you even start selling.

You will only be as good as you allow yourself to be.

If you believe that you will be average, then you will be average. If you believe that every day will be as bad as your first day, then you will suffer every day until you quit.

You escape this self-fulfilling prophecy by committing to the decision of how good you want to be. You need to commit to the manifestation and the preparation of the success that you intend to find.

You need to set your goal and imagine yourself hitting it. You need to *think about* what it will *feel like* to hit this goal. Let those *thoughts* and *emotions* motivate you to carry out the *actions* and the preparation that will get you there.

Matthew 7:7

I'm a huge believer in the law of attraction. Although it hasn't exactly been proven in the literature, I believe that you can attract realistic success by absolutely committing to it and abandoning any thoughts of turning back.

You have to think about it, imagine it, feel it, plan for it and convince yourself that it will manifest into reality.

It starts with care. Why do you care to find this success? And why do you care to not fail? Then it turns into intention. How do you intend to find this success? How will you prepare in order to attain it?

If we want to get more scientific or factual with it, then let's refer back to the cognitive triangle. Your thoughts, emotions and actions are either going to work for you or work against you.

It's your job to begin spinning your cognitive triangle in a positive direction, and then mindfully flip it whenever it starts turning negative. I cannot state the importance of positivity enough, especially when you're talking to homeowners.

You're like a magnet. You will either attract or repel homeowners with your mental state. Likewise, you will either attract or repel success with your mental state.

Controlling your cognitive triangle is essential to finding success in a performance-based environment like door-to-door sales. In order to keep your triangle spinning in a positive direction, it requires fuel, and your fuel is the underlying reason for why you care to find success.

Why do you care to persevere and attain the success that you desire? Is it money? Family? Pride? Competition? A lifestyle? Future goal? Having a clear idea is what will fuel your positivity and your grit.

Identify potential negative thoughts, emotions and actions that you're prone to experience. How are you going to flip these when the time comes? What new thought, emotion or action are you going to implement in order to re-gain positive momentum?

Are you scared of burnout, continuous rejection, the feeling of being a failure, people noticing your failure, letting someone down or becoming lazy? Figure out your biggest potential roadblock and flip it in your head *now* rather than when it hits you later on. Figure out how you're going to re-take control of your cognitive triangle.

Maybe you'll need to start taking more positive actions (workout every morning, start a gratitude journal, listen to music, call someone, etc.). The goal is to always be proactive and have a plan for how you're going to keep and recover positive momentum.

Ask yourself, what's going to keep you committed? After facing continuous rejection, what's going to motivate you?

Typically, the deeper your 'why' is (the less superficial), then the stronger it will be. But there will still be times when this isn't enough to regain positive momentum. Sometimes, it will take more than reminding yourself of the car you want to buy or the life circumstances that you want to change.

For these times, there is a stronger type of motivation that you can utilize. Although counterintuitive, it's innate to human nature. This other type of motivation is *fear*.

CHAPTER 21:

I TOLD YOU SO

Would you get up and run a mile, right now, for $100? Better yet, would you get up and run a mile, right now, or else lose $100?

Think back to the 'risk aversion' finding explained earlier. You will likely work harder to avoid your fear than you will work to achieve your goal. If your biggest fear becomes having to knock doors all day, then you will not improve, and you will definitely not hit your goal.

Regardless of how hard knocking doors becomes, you must make the fear associated with quitting/failing *bigger* than the fear of the hard work that it will take to persevere.

I want to reiterate this. You need to be crystal clear on your fear. Figure out what in your life would be more painful to go back to than the pain of grinding and improving every single day.

Setting goals is great. Deciding to commit is great. Deciding why you're committing to these goals is great. But more importantly, you need to also dig deeper and figure out what pain or fear is going to motivate you the most when you're struggling.

If you're doing door-to-door, then obviously, you're trying to make a better life for yourself. What is it about your old life that you're trying to change? What is it about your old life that would be painful to have to return to?

Figure out what your biggest fear is and use it to your advantage. Use it to motivate you when you're out of fuel.

Think of fear as an energy source that you only use when it's purposeful. Use your positivity to get you started, but understand how to conjure your fear for motivation under your own terms. I know that this is counterintuitive, so I want to give an example.

Imagine that you're running up a mountain with a group of friends who are all more conditioned than you are. You start the run, motivated to keep up with them, but after a while, you start to feel yourself slowly fall further behind.

When you're experiencing that pain and exhaustion, what's going to motivate you to keep running? What's going to motivate you to keep up with your friends?

It's probably not going to be the same motivation you started with. Rather, it will be the fear of being left behind. It will be the fear of watching all of them slowly get further and further away until they're out of sight, leaving you alone to find your way to the top.

Is your biggest fear about proving a naysayer right? Then prove them wrong. Is it about letting down your parent? Then make them proud. Is it about having to go back to your old job? Then work your ass off.

I had two big fears when starting door-to-door sales. The first fear was about having to go back to work at the psychiatric hospital. This was the motivation that helped me envision a new life that I had planned for myself.

However, it was the other fear that fueled me when I was at my lowest points. This fear was about proving a naysayer right; this naysayer happened to be one of my best friends.

In our last conversation before I left for the summer, he asked if I was even worried about how hard it would be. He asked if it was worth it to leave my job and risk failing or hating my experience.

I told him that yes, I was worried about how hard it would be. I told him that I was worried about failing, looking stupid and then hearing him say, 'I told you so.'

But then I told him that I was far more scared of what would happen if I never even tried. I told him that I was far more scared of missing out on an opportunity to change my life, and then looking back ten years down the road with regret.

In my head I knew exactly what I had committed my cognitive triangle to. And after that first summer, I ended up calling him and thanking him for doubting me. I told him that, honestly, it fueled me when I needed it the most. And the best part of all was that I got to be the one who said, 'I told you so.'

CHAPTER 22

SUMMARY

So, how good do you want to be? What level of success are you going to commit to, and how will you begin to attract it on a daily basis?

Remember the cognitive triangle - your thoughts, emotions, and actions are all interconnected. You will attract success, sales, and positive interactions by being mindful of your cognitive triangle and knowing how to control it.

Homeowners can sense your emotions. They will never want to buy from a negative person.

It's your job to understand this and manage yourself. Your inner game is just as important as the outer game with the homeowner. How you flip your negativity is just as important as how you fuel your motivation and your positivity.

Homeowners are going to actively qualify and/or stereotype you the moment they open their door, so you need to understand how to attain (and maintain) a positive snap judgment. This is how you earn the right to eventually pitch.

Just about every homeowner is going to have a negative event schema for how to deal with perceived solicitors. Therefore, your introduction needs to stack evidence that disarms this as quickly as possible. Snap judgments are made in as little as a few seconds.

Your introduction needs to be meticulously crafted, rehearsed to perfection and presented to every single homeowner. This is how you raise your odds of a positive snap judgment.

You need to perfect your body language, paraverbal communication and word choice during the first few seconds. Every detail of this first impression will be magnified in the homeowner's mind, so make sure that these details work in your favor.

Make yourself look busy when the homeowner opens their door. Make them engage with you before you look up or say anything.

Practice maintaining calm and confident body language. Keep an open posture, keep your feet firmly planted, and remember to use big smiles and head nods when it feels natural to do so. Be sure to transfer positivity with your non-verbal communication every chance you get.

Be a chameleon when you're on the doors.

Mirror homeowners' body language and overall demeanor, and remember that you can also take the initiative to sit down or lean against the side of their house once you've gotten a conversation going.

Perfect your paraverbal communication during your introduction. Slow down and lower your tone/volume of voice when you get to 'half off' or 'group rate.' Making yourself sound certain is far more important than the actual words you say.

Humans naturally qualify important information based on the way it's delivered to them. Use your certainty voice and *believe* that you're offering huge value.

As far as the words you say in your introduction, make sure that you cut out the fat. Immediately stating your name and the name of your company will sound like a stereotypical sales pitch and will often reinforce the homeowner's event schema.

Instead, get right to the point. After asking, "how are you?" or "are you the boss?" start your introduction with "the reason I'm here…" Tell the homeowner your relevance to the neighborhood and then reference some neighbors.

Utilize the recency effect by referencing the closest neighbor last. If the homeowner knows the neighbor that you mention last, then they'll be more likely to believe the first couple that you referred to.

Bring up neighbors' names later on as you explain catered details of your product/service. This bandwagon effect can easily trigger social conformity.

Cobi Beal

At the end of your introduction, after you've mentioned the discount with your perfected paraverbal communication, make sure to ask the homeowner a question.

The question at the end of your introduction should be a soft close. This will engage the homeowner and also disclose their current level of interest.

You want to pull the homeowner into a conversation. This helps you cater to the potential buyers and filter out the non-buyers.

Remind yourself that selling is a 'numbers' game. In door-to-door sales, you need to filter out the non-buyers as quickly as possible so that you can maximize the number of potential buyers you're able to talk to.

Rejection becomes a lot easier to deal with when you're actively seeking it out.

Qualification is a two-way street. Perfecting your introduction will raise your odds of being qualified positively so that you can then accurately qualify homeowners.

Perfecting your introduction will also help you challenge and de-escalate angry homeowners. Confidently referencing yourself to neighbors can often save you from being yelled at or cussed at, and will occasionally even make you a sale.

'Cognitive dissonance' can be a powerful tool during your introduction and also when you're closing. Bringing a homeowner's mistake or misjudgment to light can lead to a much more authentic conversation.

Interested homeowners will often give you a smoke-screen as an attempt to turn you down as painlessly as possible. Never give post-introduction smokescreens any weight.

Disregard smokescreens by having a one-liner prepared for the ones that are most commonly used. Then push the conversation along with another question or with a specific response. Asking another question is usually your best move.

Remember that it's your goal to generate a mutual conversation that gets the homeowner to talk and disclose useful information.

The most useful information is usually a specific 'hot button.' Your goal - after asking a question - is to listen empathetically and learn. You want to figure out how to cater your pitch to the homeowner.

What are they likely to see the most value in? What will be their biggest motivator? What will interest them enough to be willing to talk about price?

If the homeowner is interested immediately after your introduction, then you can easily transition into price; but usually, you'll need to start by building a conversation, discovering hot buttons and catering your pitch.

Homeowners typically need to have a high level of interest before they can engage in price rationalization and negotiation.

Remember that people buy with emotion and then justify with logic. Focusing on the interaction first (rapport, oxytocin, dopamine and interest) will make them more willing to justify the price.

After getting through everything, make sure to end with a hard close. Hard closes are blatantly assumptive.

This will keep you in control during the back half of the sale. The back half is when homeowners will try to re-take control, if you let them.

Being passive at this point will give control back to the homeowner. The point of a hard close is to make buying seem like the obvious answer, so if they say 'no,' then they'll usually give you a stronger and more honest reason.

Targeting their truthful hesitation will help you cater your negotiation as well as your attempts to raise their level of certainty. This is how you figure out exactly what needs to be validated and resolved.

Validation prevents you from seeming disagreeable.

This will make the homeowner more receptive to your resolve and ace. It will smoothen the transition, and it's much better than just jumping straight into a challenge or a disagreement.

Sometimes, the best form of validation can be asking a clarifying question. Taking a neutral stance and seeking to gain a better understanding of their concern will help you portray that you actually care. It will also help you learn how best to cater an ace.

Using validating questions and comments will earn you their receptiveness when you offer a price drop or a new perspective. As you incrementally drop the price, you will raise the perceived value in your offer while also triggering the law of reciprocity.

This is how you maintain a sense of pleasant persistence without seeming pushy or desperate. You need to make the homeowner feel like you're 'going out on a limb' for them rather than just saying anything to make a sale.

Your negotiation should be a double whammy. The homeowner will perceive your offer as having higher value while also feeling obliged to reciprocate the favor.

After you validate, resolve and price-drop, you should close with, "does that sound fair?" or "sound fair enough?" Continuing to use hard closes after being told 'no' can seem pushy.

If you sense that the homeowner is disengaging or feeling pushed, then change the subject. Ask them an unrelated question, and take a quick break from sales dialogue. Then slowly bring the conversation back.

The main point to remember is that homeowners will buy from the interaction, not just the pitch. You set up an effective delivery of the pitch by creating a quality experience.

This means that you should attain a positive snap judgment, implement a soft close, ask questions and listen, maintain your positive snap judgment, cater your pitch, implement a hard close, validate concerns and then leverage the law of reciprocity.

You don't need to be 'extra' in any way. You don't need to be funny or try to build fake rapport. You just need to be empathetic to the perspective of the homeowner, and generate as much positivity as you naturally can. Combine this with confidence, and you'll do just fine.

AFTERWORD

Flipping the Script is designed to help anyone who's in the door-to-door business. It's meant to give a clearer understanding of the tentative dynamic with home-owners, and to provide psychological tips and strategies that need to be incorporated into the overall pitch.

There isn't nearly enough information out there that dissects the psychology of the interaction in as much detail as door-to-door selling deserves.

Most new reps don't start out with enough of the required knowledge that it takes to find rapid success. This book can be used to significantly quicken the process. With the right insight and preparation, most new reps can build a foundation that rapidly accelerates their learning process.

The truth is that there are multiple different variables and dimensions in door-to-door sales. A single script is one-dimensional, and can't possibly embody everything there is to know.

Although a script can teach the basics of selling to highly interested homeowners, it lacks the ability to encompass the multiple different types of situations and scenarios that come with the job.

It's often been up to the sales reps to learn the psychological framework that encompasses all of the variables, and this book is designed to make that process easier. This is how you raise the odds of building positive interactions and closing more potential buyers.

If you're reading this, then you're probably selling door-to-door, or at least involved in it, and I wish you the best of luck. But truthfully, luck doesn't have anything to do with it. Luck is an excuse that people make when trying to rationalize why they can't catch a break or why they can't seem to make any progress.

Good and bad things are going to happen. Every day, you're clicking in your seat belt for an emotional roller coaster, and it's your job to stay as level-headed as possible. This is how you become a continuous learner. Doing so will be the first leap towards success, and the first step towards changing your life.

ACKNOWLEDGMENTS

To all the punchers, kickers, and biters who I worked with – thank you for teaching me how to take a hit. I can only hope that I taught you all as much as you taught me.

Thank you Brandon Wetzel for closing the deal and getting me to make a change. You're a good friend and a great leader.

For my family – thank you for your support throughout the ups and downs. I would not be who I am today without your love and guidance in my life.

Thank you Auntie Pam for your expertise during the editing process. I am beyond grateful to call you family, and friend.

Are you interested in bulk purchases of
this book for your team or company?

Contact me for a discount schedule

cdhbeal@gmail.com

...

LinkedIn – Cobi Beal

Made in the USA
Las Vegas, NV
22 April 2025

21250274R00105